CONCRETE FLATWORK

For Homeowners & Small Builders

George Garber

Schiffer Publishing Ltd

4880 Lower Valley Road · Atglen, PA · 19310

Other Schiffer Books on Related Subjects:
The Patio Portfolio: An Inspirational Design Guide. David R. Smith and Interlocking Concrete Pavement Institute. ISBN: 0-7643-2050-5. $19.95
Petite Patios & Intimate Garden Spaces. Gisela Keil, Nik Barlo, Jr., and Christa Brand. ISBN: 0-7643-2082-3. $19.95
Walkways & Drives: Design Ideas for Making Grand Entrances. Tina Skinner. ISBN: 0-7643-1360-6, $19.95

Published by Schiffer Publishing Ltd.
4880 Lower Valley Road
Atglen, PA 19310
Phone: (610) 593-1777; Fax: (610) 593-2002
E-mail: Info@schifferbooks.com

For the largest selection of fine reference books on this and related subjects, please visit our web site
at **www.schifferbooks.com**
We are always looking for people to write books on new and related subjects. If you have an idea for a book please contact us at the above address.

This book may be purchased from the publisher.
Include $5.00 for shipping.
Please try your bookstore first.
You may write for a free catalog.

In Europe, Schiffer books are distributed by
Bushwood Books
6 Marksbury Ave.
Kew Gardens
Surrey TW9 4JF England
Phone: 44 (0) 20 8392 8585; Fax: 44 (0) 20 8392 9876
E-mail: info@bushwoodbooks.co.uk
Website: www.bushwoodbooks.co.uk

693.5
GAR

Designed by RoS
Type set in Futura XBlk BTheading font/Zurich BT

ISBN: 978-0-7643-3369-9
Printed in China

CONCRETE FLATWORK

For Homeowners & Small Builders

CONCRETE

FLATWORK

Contents

FLATWORK

INTRODUCTION

The term flatwork describes the construction of any cast-in-place concrete slab that is more or less horizontal. Examples occur both outdoors and in. Outdoor slabs are often called pavements, while indoor slabs are usually known as floors.

The Flat World

When people think of flatwork around the house, sidewalks, driveways, and maybe patios come to mind. And there's nothing wrong with any of that. A well-made, traditional sidewalk is a credit to its builder, and a lot less common than you might suppose.

But the uses of flatwork go beyond those common examples. Do you play basketball or tennis? Having your own concrete court will let you play or practice whenever you want, without a trip to the gym or park. Are you building a garden shed or workshop? A smooth concrete floor will enhance your use of that building for years to come.

Concrete slabs range from the purely functional (a pad to support your recycling bin) to the highly decorative (a patio made of colored concrete with a stamped pattern). Flatwork finishes can be smooth for cleanability or rough for traction. Cast-in-place concrete blends well with other paving materials, and is often combined with asphalt, paving bricks, or concrete block pavers.

Most concrete slabs, outdoors or in, rest on the ground. Called ground-supported slabs or slabs on grade or SOGs, they are the focus of this book. There is, however a whole other category of slabs, almost all indoors, that are elevated above the ground. Resting on other building elements such as walls or columns, they are called elevated or suspended slabs. Suspended slabs are finished and cured just like their ground-supported cousins. But they are designed on fundamentally different principles. Suspended concrete floors are rare in North American houses. They are more common in commercial and industrial buildings, and in residential construction in other parts of the world.

Flatwork can be plain, like this ordinary sidewalk.

Flatwork can be more decorative. This footpath has an exposed-aggregate finish.

Is Concrete Flatwork Right For You?

Cast-in-place concrete is rarely the only possible material for a pavement or floor. Other options for outside pavements include asphalt, brick, stone, and concrete pavers, which are brick-sized blocks laid on a sand bed. For interior floors the main alternative to a concrete slab is a suspended wood floor.

My purpose here is to talk about how to make slabs out of concrete, not to try to sell you on the product. The Portland Cement Association will gladly do that. Actually there are some circumstances in which another material might be the better choice.

Are you looking for the lowest cost? Asphalt almost always beats concrete on construction cost. The long-term comparison is more complicated, however, since concrete lasts longer and needs less maintenance.

Are you looking to reduce the effect on the environment? Neither asphalt, which is made from oil, nor concrete, which requires a large amount of energy in the making of its components, is high on the list of green building materials. Perhaps you should consider stone, especially if it comes from a local quarry or has been salvaged from an old pavement. But the greenest solution is usually going to be no pavement at all.

Flatwork combines nicely with other paving materials. Here we have concrete block pavers between a concrete footpath and an asphalt driveway.

Concrete slabs hold up in harsh environments.

Cast-in-place
concrete mixes here
with block pavers.

As versatile as concrete
is, it is not the only paving
material you should
consider. This asphalt path
in a city park undoubtedly
cost less than concrete.

Are You Right For Concrete Flatwork?

I wrote this book for two groups: homeowners who want to do their own concrete flatwork, and small general builders who, while not specializing in flatwork, may need to do some of it from time to time. If you've read this far, you may already belong to one of those groups. Or you may still wonder whether flatwork is something you can or should take on.

First the bad news: concrete work is hard. In a world where power tools have eased many tasks, the construction of small slabs is still an old-fashioned job that will put sweat on your brow and blisters on your hands. If you choose to mix your own concrete, the workload gets even heavier. And the physical labor is only half of it. Concrete work occurs under intense time pressure. Once cement meets water, it starts an unstoppable chemical reaction that will result in the concrete becoming rock-hard in a few hours. Those few hours are all the time you will ever have to place, compact, strike off, and finish the concrete. Not only do you have to work hard, but sometimes you have to work fast.

But there's good news too. Small-scale flatwork doesn't require expensive tools or skills that take years to master. It's a field where an ambitious beginner can do good work. If you learn the basics (this book is a start), work hard, and think carefully about every step, you can produce a slab superior to what you'd get from a concrete contractor out of the phone book.

Small-scale flatwork still relies on hand tools and hard work.

Getting Information

If you're smart, you'll rely on more than just this book. I don't have all the answers. Be wary, though, because there's a lot of bum information out there, especially on the internet. Most web sites that offer help on flatwork are really ads. You can learn from ads, of course, but don't forget their aim. It is generally not to enable you to build the best slab at the lowest price.

Turning to more objective sources like the American Concrete Institute and Concrete Construction magazine, you'll find plenty of information on concrete in general and flatwork in particular. Some of it is useful. But you'll find that a lot of it doesn't apply to the kind of flatwork you have in mind. It doesn't apply because concrete slab construction has, in recent decades, branched into two increasingly separate forms divided by size.

Reading books and magazines about slab construction, you'd think everyone was finishing concrete with machines like this double-rotor trowel machine. In contrast, you are more likely to be finishing by hand, or with a single-rotor, walk-behind machine.

One branch includes big industrial floors, slabs in high-rise buildings, and concrete highways. The other branch includes the sidewalks, driveways, and garage floors that form the subject of this book. Up to the last quarter of the twentieth century, the two branches were not very distinct. Big slabs and small slabs were built in more or less the same way. Naturally a contractor laying a big warehouse floor used more workers and placed more concrete per day than a homeowner replacing a sidewalk. But the materials and methods in both cases were similar.

That has changed. The big contractors who do big slabs have adopted costly, high-powered machines to do much of the work. Highway builders use motorized paving trains that place and finish the concrete almost automatically. There is hardly a hand tool to be seen. Industrial floor slabs today are placed by a laser-guided power screed and finished with twin-rotor power trowels. The equipment on a single job can easily cost over half a million dollars. To pay for that equipment, the amount of concrete placed per day has steadily risen. When I started out in 1979 a big industrial floor contractor might place 10,000 sq ft (1,000 sq m) a day. Now a normal day's work is more like 35,000 sq ft (3,300 sq m), and pours of 100,000 sq ft (9,300 sq m) aren't that unusual.

In contrast, small-scale jobs haven't changed much. Sidewalks and patios are still built by small crews using hand tools.

If you want to learn the small-scale side of the business, you won't get much out of visiting a modern, high-production slab pour (assuming they even let you in, which is doubtful). By the same token, you will find that many of the published articles and books on modern concrete construction have little to offer you.

So where can you learn, beyond this book? One place is at somebody else's house. If you ask around, you can probably find a friend, relative, or neighbor who wants to put in a concrete slab and would love some free help. You'll learn a lot if you volunteer, even if the other people on the job don't know much more than you. Failing that, the best course is to start out on a small, unimportant slab and learn from trial and error.

In recent decades large-scale slab construction has deviated more and more from small-scale flatwork. Industrial floor contractors routinely use big, expensive machines like this laser screed.

Laser-screed controls. Don't try this at home.

CONCRETE

A three-person crew is the practical minimum for a driveway or patio, especially if you use ready-mix concrete.

It's hard to have too much help when spreading concrete.

FLATWORK

CHAPTER 1

Getting Ready

Before you start building your slab, give some thought to a few background issues.

Hands

Concrete flatwork is not for soloists. You can frame a house or shingle a roof on your own and get great results; the only drawback will be a slow rate of progress. But that doesn't work with concrete, which follows its own schedule. You have just a few hours to get the concrete on the ground, strike it off, and finish it before it gets hard. You need enough willing workers to accomplish all that.

Two people can do a sidewalk, though it goes better with three. A driveway or a garage floor really needs three or more. If you can't persuade your friends to help (or maybe you just want to make sure they remain friends), consider hiring a day laborer or two. Most good-sized American towns have a spot where workers wait for day jobs. You may have to ask around to find it, though.

If you absolutely must work alone, you need to make a few adjustments. Forget ready-mix concrete; you can't handle a full truckload of it and short loads cost too much. Mix your concrete on site and keep the batches small. Watch the slab width, too. Sidewalks are OK, but when placing a driveway or patio you should divide it into two or more narrow strips. A Hollywood driveway is a good choice because it always comes in two strips, each strip even narrower than a sidewalk.

Safety

You can get hurt around concrete. Though staying safe is mainly a matter of common sense, concrete work involves a few special risks that may not be obvious.

Risks

Concrete is heavy, and lifting it can lead to back trouble and other injuries. A cubic foot of concrete weighs about 150 pounds; a bushel basket of the stuff (not that you'd carry it that way) weighs 190 pounds. A standard bag of cement weighs 94 pounds. If you live where metric is spoken, you may be looking at 50 kg bags, though there has recently been a move toward smaller ones.

Maybe you can handle loads like those without any trouble. But even people who are fit and healthy can't always lift a hundred pounds. If you, like me, know that you will never win a weightlifting contest, the answer is easy. Limit the load. For example you can fit over 300 pounds of wet concrete into a wheelbarrow. You can, but maybe you shouldn't. Fill it halfway and save your back. If you have to move bagged cement or concrete mix, use a hand truck.

Watch out for ready-mix trucks. Normally it's a good idea to stay clear of any big machine in motion, but with ready-mix trucks you can't always do that. You may have to guide a truck driver as she backs into a tight spot, and you have to stand near the truck chutes to place the concrete where you want it. Be careful, and keep an eye out for others working or standing nearby. The chutes are especially dangerous because they are both heavy and hinged. You may need to handle them, but keep your hands away from the hinges lest you lose a finger.

A more insidious danger lurks in the concrete itself: chemical burns. Fresh concrete is alkaline and caustic. It burns skin, but not right away—that's the insidious part. If you stick your bare hand in concrete you won't feel any pain, and if you pull it out right away you won't suffer any harm. But leave that hand in concrete for an hour, and you'll be paying a visit to the emergency room. The trick, then, is to avoid prolonged contact with wet concrete. The risk is greatest in cool, damp weather when clothes get soaked with concrete juice and don't dry out.

How do you prevent chemical burns? Wearing waterproof clothes from head to toe would do the job, but nobody does that. A more sensible approach is to wear rubber boots if you know you'll be standing in wet concrete, leather boots if you think you can stay dry, and to consider rubber gloves. Then you try to keep the rest of your body more or less concrete-free. If you get really drenched—say, from falling headlong into the pour—take the wet clothes off right away and rinse off with water. In a pinch, you can use the hose on the ready-mix truck. Taking a cold shower in public isn't on anyone's to-do list, but it beats second-degree burns.

The risk continues for a while even after the concrete has set. If you wet-saw or wet-grind concrete when it is a day or two old, the resulting slurry can still burn skin. However, fully cured, dry concrete is safe, and indeed is about as harmless and non-toxic as any material found around the house.

Protective Gear

The safety helmet, or hard hat, has become the symbol of the modern construction worker. But it's one item you don't necessarily need for concrete flatwork unless someone is working overhead. Other forms of protection matter more. Amateurs and small contractors often use little or no safety gear, but they also get hurt at higher rates than the employees of big construction firms, who tend to have strict rules on this subject. Let's look at what some of those firms require, from the forehead down.

Safety glasses protect the eyes from flying objects. Concrete work might not look like the sort of activity that puts eyes at risks, but it is. The mere action of wet concrete falling off the chute of a ready-mix truck can send bits shooting through the air, head high. Pumping increases the risk. And jobs often include the use of tools like electric saws that call for eye protection.

Ear guards—ear plugs or muffs—reduces long-term hearing loss. Ready-mix trucks, power trowels, and concrete saws all make enough noise to cause damage. You probably won't notice the effect of a day or two around such noisy machines, but in the long run it's your exposure to all loud sounds, from whatever source, that determines how your hearing holds up.

Consider dust masks if you will be dealing with dry cement. Cement dust will be flying around if you mix on site. It probably won't be an issue if you buy ready-mix.

Reflective vests make you visible after sunset (or before dawn). Wearing one is a good idea if your job runs early or late and is located close to the street or road.

Gloves are optional. If you choose to wear them, stay away from lightweight cloth versions. When concrete juice soaks them, the corrosive effect on your skin will be worse than if you went barehanded. Leather or rubberized gloves are safer.

Knee pads aren't always considered safety-related, but they can eliminate a lot of discomfort. If you don't have knee pads you will be tempted to bend down when working low, and that's hard on the back. Or you'll squat, and that's hard on the knees. Kneeling is the best way to get down close to the concrete surface, and pads let you do it with ease.

Rubber boots are essential if you have to stand in wet concrete, and the taller the better. If you plan to stay out of the concrete, as you usually can on narrow pours such as sidewalks, leather boots work fine. I've met a few concrete finishers who switch to sneakers when they have to walk on the slab for floating and trowelling. Soft shoes are a little less likely to leave marks that can't be trowelled out.

You might notice that some photos in this book show workers conspicuously not wearing recommended protective gear. I photograph people on real-world job sites, and in the real world people don't always take the precautions they should. But those people sometimes get hurt; you don't have to be one of them.

The Law

You can't, in most places, build whatever you want. The law regulates most kinds of flatwork. Oh, you can put down a few square feet to set your garbage can on and not worry about the building inspector giving you grief. But beyond that you should at least ask around to see what local rules apply, and which ones are actually enforced. You will probably find different regulations for indoor and outdoor slabs.

A floor slab within a house or garage is normally subject to your locality's building code. Depending on where you live, you may have to get a building permit and schedule an inspection before pouring concrete. The strictest rules apply to suspended slabs—those that rest on walls or beams and have empty space below.

Exterior concrete tends to be less regulated, unless it's a sidewalk in the public right of way. In that case expect a very specific set of rules telling you where the sidewalk must go, how wide and thick it must be, and sometimes even what concrete mix to use. On top of all that, you may have to deal with ADAAG—the Americans with Disabilities Act Accessibility Guidelines (see sidebar on page 102).

The law generally gives you a lot of latitude when it comes to driveways (except where they cross sidewalks), patios, and sports surfaces. There is one area, however, where the regulation of exterior slabs is increasing, and that is the matter of water runoff. More and more towns are limiting the percentage of a property that can be covered by impervious materials like asphalt and ordinary concrete. Narrow paths may be exempt, but driveways and patios usually aren't. Some governments don't apply the limits to the yards of detached houses, but that may change. If you find yourself bumping against the limits, consider pervious concrete made without fine aggregate. Pervious concrete lets water pass through into the ground.

When checking the rules, don't just look at government regulations. Nowadays over half the houses built in the United States are subject to covenants—private agreements that limit what you can do on your property. Many covenants restrict concrete paving. And in some neighborhoods covenants are enforced more strictly than municipal laws.

Pervious Pavements

Think you'd like a concrete pavement that lets rain pass through? You can have one if you make it with no-fines concrete.

Pervious pavements have been around for decades, but interest in them is growing as people become more concerned with water runoff. Nowadays many local governments limit the amount of impervious pavement allowed on a piece of land. Pavements made of no-fines concrete may be exempt from those limits, since they let water percolate.

Pervious pavement also makes sense if you want to prevent water from ponding but can't or don't want to slope the slab to shed water.

No-fines concrete

As the name suggests, no-fines concrete contains no fine aggregate. You make it with a narrowly graded coarse aggregate, cement, and water. The cement paste coats the coarse aggregate particles so they will stick together, but it does not fill all the gaps. The result is concrete full of holes. It looks something like regular concrete with an exposed-aggregate finish.

If you hire a contractor to lay a pervious pavement, you may have to pay a big premium. But no-fines concrete isn't harder to work with than normal concrete. It's just different.

Many of the standard concrete rules don't apply when you take out the fines. To start with, you don't want a normal coarse aggregate with a broad range of particle sizes. It's better to use a so-called single-size aggregate in which almost all the particles are about the same size. The size can be anything from 3/8 in. (10 mm) up to 1 in. (25 mm). Many people think the smaller rocks look better. The appearance of the

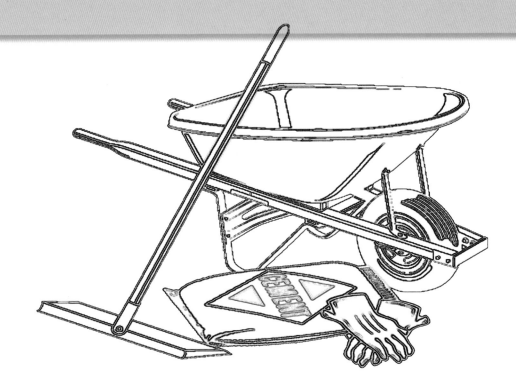

aggregate matters since it will be exposed to view. Crushed rock and rounded natural gravel both work, but they look different.

Ready-mix companies can supply a no-fines mix, but don't be surprised if your local plant doesn't have much experience in this field. You can also mix it yourself. The British Cement Association recommends a 1:4 mix—one part cement to four parts coarse aggregate, by volume. Take great care with water, adding just enough to create a cement paste that coats all the stone. If you live where temperatures fall below freezing, use an air-entraining admixture.

Some people add just a bit of sand to the mix—say, 100 lb per cubic yard (60 kg per cubic metre). Strictly speaking, we can't call the result no-fines concrete, but it's still full of holes and still pervious.

Normal concrete is usually struck off level with the side forms, but that won't work with a no-fines mix. Strike it off about 1/2 in. (12 mm) high. An easy way to do that is to tack wood battens to the tops of the forms.

After striking off, peel off the battens and compact the concrete with a heavy roller. A steel pipe will work—and the bigger and heavier, the better. Some people stand on the pipe and work it along like lumberjacks on a floating log. That's both effective and fun, but I advise carrying a long prop so you can keep your balance.

The roller not only compacts the concrete, but provides most of the finish. Though you might want to touch up an edge with a hand float, for most part floats and trowels are neither needed nor effective on no-fines concrete.

One last thing: dirt and organic debris can plug the holes in no-fines concrete. An occasional pass with a vacuum cleaner will help keep your pervious pavement pervious.

Where To Shop

You won't find one business that sells everything you need for concrete flatwork, unless you're putting in a tiny slab and using bagged concrete mix. Then you could get it all at a general building supply store.

You may need to deal with:

• hardware stores for hand tools, nails, polyethylene sheet, and concrete sealers
• lumberyards for formwork
• general building supply stores for all the above, along with cement, bagged concrete mix, reinforcing steel
• ready-mix concrete suppliers for concrete and admixtures
• stone and sand dealers for sub-base materials and aggregates
• equipment rental stores for hand tools, steel forms, concrete mixers, wheelbarrows, and buggies

FLATWORK

CHAPTER 2

Principles Of Slab Design

Every concrete slab has a designer. If you're building a small slab around the house, chances are that designer is you.

But don't let that scare you. Slab design need not involve formal drawings and complex calculations—though it can, if that's what you like. What it does involve is a series of decisions. The designer has to answer these questions:

Will the ground support the slab?
Does the slab need a vapor barrier?
How thick will the slab be?
What kind of concrete will you use?
How will the slab be reinforced?
How will the slab be jointed to control cracks?

Before we get to those questions, I want to issue a warning. With few exceptions, my comments in this chapter apply only to ground-supported slabs. They do not apply to suspended, elevated slabs. You can design a ground-supported slab like a driveway with common sense and the information in this book. Even if you make a big mistake, you aren't likely to hurt anyone. But suspended slabs are another story. They can fall down and kill people. If you are tackling a suspended slab, hire a structural engineer to design it. Or—if you are absolutely sure you understand what you are doing—you may be able to use a standard design that fully meets your local building code. Either way, you'll need more than this book to do the job safely.

Subgrade & Sub-base

A ground-supported slab depends on, well, the ground—which is called the subgrade when it forms part of a floor or pavement. But subgrades vary.

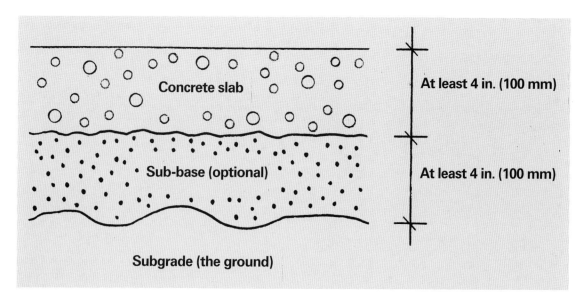

Components of a concrete slab

How do you find what kind of ground you have? You can hire a geotechnical engineer to survey it for you. And if you're building a house, especially one in an area known for problem soil, you should consider doing so. But nobody does that for a sidewalk or patio. Another option is to ask the neighbors. If the neighborhood has serious issues such as highly expansive clay or sinkholes, people will have stories to tell.

The last resort is to start digging and see for yourself. As a general rule, the finer the grain of the base material, the more likely it is to give trouble. Gravel is great. Sand is OK. But silt and clay, which consist of much smaller particles than sand grains, make poorer bases. And keep an eye out for trash that would suggest the site has been filled.

If you're blessed with gravel or sand, all you need do is grade it and tamp it. But what if you're not so lucky?

Success is still possible, but you have to make adjustments. The first step is to add a sub-base—a layer of granular fill between subgrade and slab. A sub-base offers several benefits. It helps distribute loads, insulates the slab from ground movement, and can make the slab thickness more uniform. A sub-base should be at least 4 in. (100 mm) thick, but consider making it thicker if your subgrade has unusual problems.

However, some subgrade problems are so severe that even a generous sub-base won't save the day. Problems in that category include extremely soft soil, sinkholes, and expansive clay (see sidebar). Those cases call for more drastic measures.

One answer is to remove the bad material and replace it with better stuff. Another answer is to use a generous amount of steel reinforcement in the slab. The reinforcement won't stop subgrade movement or slab cracking, but it will help keep your slab in one piece.

Vapor Barriers

Stop moisture, in the form of water vapor, from rising from the ground into the concrete. Some people call them vapor retarders instead of barriers, on the grounds that they don't block all the moisture. The most common material is polyethylene sheet. It usually goes directly under the slab, but some people prefer to put it under the sub-base instead.

Not every slab gets a vapor barrier. The general rule is that outdoors slabs don't need them, while indoor slabs do.

Remember that the membrane's purpose is not to protect the concrete (which water doesn't harm), but to stop moisture from damaging things like carpets and cardboard boxes that sit on top of the slab. That explains why outdoor slabs rarely need vapor barriers; why worry about ground moisture when the top of the slab sits out in the open, exposed to whatever moisture falls from the sky? In contrast, building codes often require vapor barriers under indoor floor slabs unless you have a good argument for leaving them out. In some arid regions the local builders omit vapor barriers even in houses, but I wouldn't follow that unless you know it's been done successfully in your neighborhood.

Slab Thickness

Slab thickness determines how much load a slab can take without breaking. Thickness is not the only factor; concrete strength matters too, as does the quality of the ground below the slab. But slab thickness is the big one. If you double the concrete

Do You Have Swelling Soil?

Most soils expand when they get wet and shrink when they dry out. Certain soils known as expansive clays take that behavior to extremes. Where expansive clays are thick, the surface of the ground can move up and down by many inches as its moisture content changes. The risk is greatest in places that have distinct wet and dry seasons. Swelling soil destroys concrete slabs and even wrecks whole buildings. It is one of the hardest challenges you can face in planning a pavement or floor.

How will you know if your site contains expansive clay? Try asking around. If the problem is severe, it will probably be common knowledge in the neighborhood. Or look for visual clues, such as sidewalks tilted at crazy angles or masonry walls with huge cracks.

Though expansive clays affect both indoor and outdoor slabs, it's the indoor slabs that cause the most concern because their failure can make a building unusable.

There are several ways to save flatwork from the ravages of swelling soil, though not all are suitable for every job, and some will cost you an arm and a leg. You can:

- Dig out the offending clay and replace it with stable fill. This works well, but in some cases a huge amount of material needs to be removed.
- Protect floor slabs from excessive moisture with wide roof overhangs and good site drainage.
- Avoid placing slabs near big trees that can suck moisture out from under the concrete.
- Use heavy reinforcement in the slab.
- Post-tension the slab.
- Support the slab on piles that penetrate the expansive clay.

Post-tensioning is common for house slabs in Texas and Louisiana. Australians, in contrast, tend to favor roof overhangs and limits on planting.

strength, the slab's load capacity also doubles. But if you double the slab thickness, capacity goes up about four times.

The engineers who design heavy industrial floors work hard on slab thickness analysis. They examine loads in detail and run computer programs to come up with the most economic combination of slab thickness and concrete strength.

But you don't need to worry about all that, because the loads you deal with will be light. Indeed, if you ran the numbers on a footpath or patio, you might conclude that a 2-in. (50-mm) slab would suffice. However, long experience has shown that 2-in. slabs don't fare well, no matter how light the loads.

So most slabs around the house are 4 in. (100 mm) thick, not because calculations prove it's the right number, but rather because it's worked for many decades. Sidewalks, driveways, patios, and house slabs are all 4 in. (100 mm) thick, most of the time.

I could almost tell you to make your slabs 4 in. (100 mm) thick and be done with it. You might, however want a thicker slab in a driveway that will have to support trucks. Some local codes call for 6 in. (150 mm) in driveways and where sidewalks cross driveways. A few towns even require 5-in. (125-mm) sidewalks, though I wonder how strictly they enforce that rule.

You may get advice that a 3-in. (75-mm) slab is OK for footpaths. And perhaps it is, most of the time. But I recommend against it for two reasons. First, you can rarely be sure a pavement will be forever limited to foot traffic. Sooner or later someone may need to drive a truck over it, and when that day comes you will be glad to have a thicker slab. Second—and this is the more important reason—slabs aren't really as thick as they are designed to be. A nominal 4-in. (100-mm) slab can easily go down to 3 in. (75 mm) in spots. (There will be some 5-in. (125-mm) spots too, but no one worries about them.) You can live with that, but if you aim for 3 in. (75 mm) and get some 2-in. (50-mm) spots, that's a problem.

Concrete Strength & Other Properties

Concrete is defined by its compressive strength --its ability to resist crushing force. That can be misleading, since compressive strength does not, taken on it own, have much to do with whether a concrete slab succeeds or fails. Other properties, especially shrinkage and workability, matter more. But that doesn't change the fact that compressive strength is the property almost everyone focuses on, so we can't ignore it.

Compressive Strength

To measure compressive strength, you put a sample of concrete in a cabibrated press and apply force till the sample is crushed. The force is measured in pounds per square inch (psi) or megapascals (MPa). Normal concrete breaks between 2000 and 6000 psi (15 and 40 MPa) when tested in this way. When people talk about "a 3000-psi mix" or "30-MPa concrete" without further explanation, you can safely assume they are describing compressive strength. And when someone mentions "3000-pound" concrete, it doesn't mean the concrete weighs 3000 lb. It means the concrete has a 3000-psi compressive strength.

Concrete's strength is measured by casting small cylinders like these, and then breaking them in a calibrated press.

It's unlikely any concrete you pour will actually be tested for compressive strength. But you should still be familiar with the concept, since you may need to order ready-mix concrete by compressive strength, and books and articles about flatwork may recommend a specific strength for a project.

I'll make it easy. For almost any piece of flatwork around the house, you won't go wrong with 3500-psi (25-MPa) concrete. It's readily available from ready-mix plants, and it's what you are supposed to get if you use bagged concrete mix and follow all instructions.

Exceptions? I can think of two good reasons to specify higher strength. If the local code requires a higher strength, you need to follow that unless you are prepared to fight for an exception (or want to risk breaking the rules). And if you are building something designed by a structural engineer, you need to follow his or her recommendations for concrete strength.

There is an argument for lower strength, too, but it's less persuasive. If you reduce the strength by cutting cement, you get concrete that shrinks less and therefore cracks less—however counterintuitive that may seem. That's good, but the reduction in cement makes the concrete harder to finish, and finish is essential in flatwork. Strengths below 3500 psi (25 MPa) make sense in some concrete structures, but I'd avoid them in slabs that need a good finish because they might not contain enough cement.

Don't worry about strength if you are mixing concrete on site. The commonly-used recipes all contain enough cement for both adequate compressive strength and a good finish.

Drying Shrinkage

All concrete shrinks as it dries, but some concrete mixes shrink more than others. Since drying shrinkage makes slabs crack and curl, try to find a mix that will shrink less, to the extent you have a choice.

Unlike compressive strength, drying shrinkage is rarely tested. If you call the local ready-mix plant and ask for shrinkage data, you probably won't get any. (If by chance you do get some data, look for a mix that shows 28-day drying shrinkage of 0.035% or less.)

Unless you are lucky enough to live in an enlightened area where the ready-mix plants supply concrete with known shrinkage, you won't be sure you have a low-shrinkage mix. But here are some steps to better the odds:

Use bigger rocks—in other words, a coarse aggregate with a bigger top size. Much coarse aggregate tops out at about 3/4 in. (20 mm). Try to get aggregate that goes up to 1-1/2 in. (40 mm). But don't go far above that, because then you will have trouble in placing and striking off.

Use clean, washed aggregates.

If you have a choice between crushed rock and rounded natural gravel, choose the crushed rock. It may cost more. In most markets you don't get to choose, though.

Use the least cement that will give the strength and workability you need. If you are mixing on site, a 1:2:4 mix will, all else being equal, shrink less than a 1:2:3.

Use the least water that will give the workability you need. But don't go too far and leave the mix so stiff you can't handle it properly. Workability matters as much as shrinkage, so you have to find the right balance.

Workability

This is the ease with which concrete can be placed, compacted, and struck off. Highly workable concrete is called wet. Concrete of low workability is called stiff or dry. Workability is closely related to finishability—the easy with which a concrete slab can be floated, trowelled, and broomed.

Workability is not just a matter of judgement. It can be quantified, and by far the most common measure is the slump test. You start with a cone-shaped mold 12 in. (300 mm) tall, open at top and bottom. You fill the mold with fresh concrete and then gently raise the mold. No longer confined by the sheet metal, the concrete slumps. The amount by which it slumps is the measure of its workability. If the concrete didn't settle at all, that would be a zero slump. If it poured out like water, that would be a 12-in. (300-mm) slump. Real-world concrete slumps range from 1 in. (25 mm) to 8 in. (200 mm).

I describe the slump test not because you will have to perform it, but because understanding can help you communicate with your concrete supplier. When you order ready-mix concrete, the salesperson may ask you what slump you want. When the concrete truck arrives on site, the driver may tell you what slump he's running. It will be a guess, but an informed one. And the driver may offer to add water to raise the slump to the value you seek.

What slump should you ask for, then? It's hard to know in advance exactly what will work best. But since the ideal slump usually falls between 4 and 6 in. (100 and 150 mm), you could start by splitting the difference and requesting 5 in. (125 mm).

If the slump is too low, you won't be able to compact the concrete well and the surface will be hard to close and finish. If the slump is too high, the mix may segregate (this means the coarse and fine materials will separate from each other) and finishing will take a long time.

Some people may tell you to keep the slump as low as you can because high slumps lead to weak concrete and high shrinkage. There's some truth to that, but only a little.

While several factors affect workability, water content heads the list. A small amount of extra water greatly increases concrete's workability. That's why adjustments to workability are usually made by changing the amount of water added to the mix. If concrete is too stiff, add a little water and mix it in thoroughly.

Reinforcement

is something (usually steel) imbedded in the concrete that serves to resist certain stresses that the concrete cannot handle. It may be the most misunderstood part of a concrete slab.

If you ask the average person what reinforcement does for concrete, you are likely to get one of two answers. It makes the concrete stronger, or it prevents cracks. But neither statement is true except in very restricted senses.

The purpose of reinforcement is to resist tensile stresses—forces that want to pull the slab apart—after the concrete has cracked. Some concrete elements—long beams, for example—are subject to large tensile stresses and are designed to crack under those stresses. Such elements need plenty of reinforcement to keep from coming apart after they have cracked.

Ground-supported slabs are different. If laid on good ground and properly jointed, they get only modest tensile stress. Concrete can resist that stress by itself. That's why you can build slabs with no reinforcement.

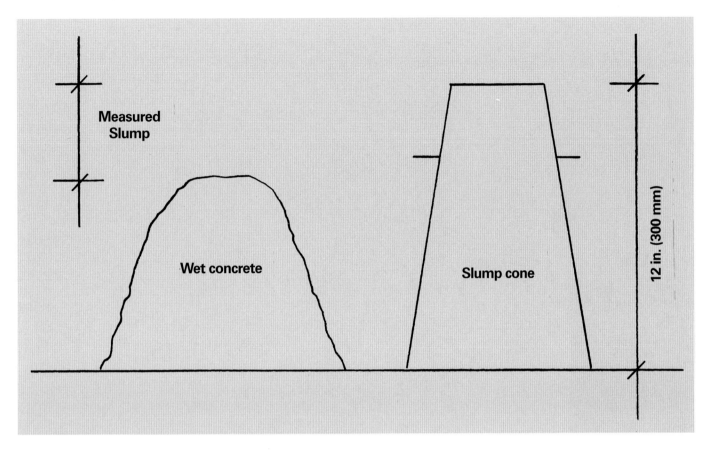

Measured Slump

Wet concrete

Slump cone

12 in. (300 mm)

The slump test is a way to check concrete workability.

Concrete's workability is defined by its slump. A metal cone is filled with wet concrete and then gently lifted. The concrete settles or slumps as the cone is removed. For most flatwork you want something close to a 5-in. (125-mm) slump.

Does that mean we can forget about reinforcing flatwork? Not quite. Reinforcement makes sense in certain situations. Brittle floorcoverings like ceramic tile can break if a crack in the underlying slab grows too wide. Reinforcement won't stop the crack, but it can limit the crack's width, saving the tile. If you are building on very poor soil where a lot of settlement or heaving can occur, reinforcement can keep cracks and joints from faulting. (Faulting occurs when one side of a crack or joint becomes higher than the other, leaving a step.)

And don't forget that the unreinforced-slab option applies only at ground level. Elevated slabs are designed on different principles and always contain some kind of reinforcement.

Once you decide to reinforce a slab, you have two big decisions to make. What form will the reinforcement take, and how much will you use?

Kinds Of Reinforcement

Reinforcing steel comes in three forms: wire mesh, deformed bars (rebar), and fibers. Wire mesh consists of steel wires laid out in a grid, with all intersections welded. It comes in a wide range of wire sizes and spacings, but only the lightest gauges are commonly used in light-duty flatwork. In the United States, general building supply stores usually only stock so-called 10-gauge mesh, officially known as 6x6, W1.4xW1.4. Wire mesh works best when it's close to the slab's surface, but if it's too close it will affect the finish. A depth of 1-1/2 to 2 in. (40 to 50 mm) is about right. If you want wire mesh in the right spot (why use it otherwise?), support it on concrete bricks or special devices, called chairs, made for that purpose. Many pros don't do that. They lay the mesh on the ground and just pull it up into the wet concrete, hoping it will stay up. The key word there is hoping. Time and again tests have found wire mesh on the bottom of the slab. They might as well have left it on the truck.

Reinforcing steel won't prevent cracks, but it limits their width. This is a hairline crack in a heavily-reinforced slab.

Deformed bars are steel rods with bumps to lock them into the concrete. The sizes you are most likely to use are #3 (3/8 in. diameter) and #4 (1/2 in. diameter). The metric equivalents are 10M (10 mm diameter) and 12M (12 mm diameter). A reasonable bar pattern for a 4-in. (100-mm) slab consists of #3 (10M) bars spaced 15 in. (380 mm) on center, running both the length and width of the slab. To maintain the grid, tie the bar intersections with steel wire. Like wire mesh, deformed bars should be chaired up so they stay 1-1/2 to 2 in. (40 to 50 mm) below the slab surface.

Steel fibers are thin wires from 1 to 2 in. (25 to 50 mm) long. They are mixed into the wet concrete and are supposed to be distributed throughout the slab.

Quantities

In deciding how much reinforcement to use, and in comparing different patterns, the number to look at is the cross-sectional area of steel divided by the cross-sectional area of the slab, expressed as a percentage. The formula below will work with wire mesh and rebar of any size:

$R = 100[(D/2)^2]\pi / (TS)$

Where:

R = steel cross-sectional area as a percentage of slab cross-sectional area

D = diameter of individual wire or rebar

T = slab thickness

S = wire or rebar spacing, center to center

D, T, and S must all be measured in the same units.

The ubiquitous 10-gauge mesh provides 0.06% steel, if your slab is 4 in. (100 mm) thick. Increase the slab thickness to 6 in. (150 mm), and the same mesh give you only 0.04%. If you go up to 6x6, W2.9xW2.9 mesh, the steel percentage rises to 0.12% in a 4-in. (100-mm slab).

Light-gauge wire
mesh

#3 rebar

The table below shows how much reinforcement you get from #3 and #4 bars at various spacings, assuming the slab thickness remains 4 in. (100 mm).

Spacing	#3 bars	#4 bars
6 in.	0.46%	0.82%
12 in.	0.23%	0.41%
15 in.	0.18%	0.33%
18 in.	0.15%	0.27%
24 in.	0.12%	0.20%

And here's the table for metric rebar, assuming a 100-mm slab thickness:

Spacing	10-mm bars	12-mm bars
150 mm	0.52%	0.75%
300 mm	0.26%	0.38%
380 mm	0.21%	0.30%
500 mm	0.16%	0.23%
600 mm	0.13%	0.19%

Now comes the big question: what percentage of steel do you want? There seem to be as many answers to that question as there are engineers designing slabs. But here are some guidelines.

If you want to limit all cracks to a barely visible hairline, without any limit on slab length or distance between joints, use at least 0.5%. Forget about accomplishing that with standard mesh; it's far too light. You'll need rebar. If your slab is 4 in. thick, you can get 0.5% with #3 bars spaced 5-1/2 in. on center, or #4s at 10 in. (Metric equivalents would be 10-mm bars at 150 mm or 12-mm bars at 225 mm). Such heavy reinforcement is rare in small-scale flatwork, and almost certainly more than you need. But it will give you a slab that's close to bulletproof.

Following the traditional rule for minimum reinforcement in suspended slabs, some designers aim for 0.18% steel. That's still more than standard mesh will give you. In a 4-in. (100-mm) slab you can reach 0.18% with #3s at 15 in., or with 10-mm bars at 430 mm.

In modern large-scale floors it has become common to use about 0.12% steel. That's enough to limit crack width, but not so much that it locks up the control joints and stops them from relieving stresses as they are meant to. Now we are finally down in the range where wire mesh becomes an option. If you can find 6x6, W2.9xW2.9 mesh, it will give you 0.12% in a 4-in. (100-mm) slab. Or you could use #3s at 24 in., or 10-mm bars at 650 mm.

You may have noticed that the common 10-gauge mesh, available at any general building-supply house, falls short of all the recommended percentages I have mentioned. Is there a place for it at all? Well, I wouldn't use it. The light-gauge mesh provides only 0.06% steel in a 4-in. (100-mm) slab. I say if you can live with that, you can live with 0.00%—no steel at all. There is, however, a counter-argument that even a little reinforcement is better than none.

Reinforcement usually forms a grid with equal amounts of steel in two perpendicular directions. But it doesn't have to. A long, narrow slab may need substantial reinforcement running the long way, but little or none running the short way. With rebar you can easily

Spot reinforcement could have stopped this crack from widening.

use different spacings, and even different bar sizes, in the two directions. In theory you can do that with wire mesh as well, but mesh made in that way may be hard to find, at least in North America.

Where do steel fibers fit into all this? Comparing fibers to wire mesh and rebar is tricky, because fibers run in all directions while the alternatives are all more-or-less horizontal. Some fibers end up vertical and don't do much to control ordinary cracks. According to Mike McPhee of Fibercon International (a steel-fiber manufacturer), the following steps offer a conservative way to compare fibers to wire mesh or rebar:

1. Start with the amount of conventional reinforcement you would use, expressed as a percentage of the slab's cross-sectional area: pounds per cubic yard or kilograms per cubic metre.
2. If working in US Customary units, multiply the percentage by 307. This will give you the equivalent amount of steel fiber, in pounds per cubic yard of concrete.
3. If working in metric units, multiply the percentage by 181. This will give you the equivalent amount of steel fiber, in kilograms per cubic metre of concrete.

By that method, to get the equivalent of 0.12% reinforcement would take 37 lb of fiber per cubic yard of concrete (22 kg per cubic metre).

Spot Reinforcement

So far we have been talking about reinforcement that runs the full length and width of the slab. There is another way to use reinforcing steel, and that is to put short lengths of it where you expect cracks.

The best candidate for spot reinforcement is the re-entrant corner. A couple of #4 (12-mm) bars, 18 in. (450 mm) long, placed diagonally at the corner will stop any crack from widening.

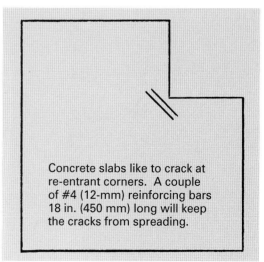

Concrete slabs like to crack at re-entrant corners. A couple of #4 (12-mm) reinforcing bars 18 in. (450 mm) long will keep the cracks from spreading.

31

Control Joints

Concrete likes to crack. If you spend any time around construction people you will hear the jokes. Every concrete truck has a crack in it. Or there are three things you can count on about concrete: it's grey, it gets hard, and it cracks. The jokes aren't literally true, but they get close.

Why do concrete slabs crack? The main culprit is shrinkage. All concrete starts out wet and shrinks as it dries. In addition to that drying shrinkage, many concrete slabs are subject to big temperature swings that cause even more shrinkage. (Temperature changes cause expansion as well as shrinkage, but the expansion's not a problem.)

Slabs also crack because of things that happen underneath. Ground frost and growing tree roots can break concrete. So can consolidation of the soil, and soil swelling and shrinking due to moisture changes.

Very small slabs—up to 4x4 ft (1.2x1.2 m)—rarely crack from any of those causes. Somewhat bigger slabs - up to about 15x15 ft (4.5x4.5 m) can remain crack-free if they are free to shrink and don't suffer from subgrade problems.

Joints divide bigger slabs into small pieces that are less likely to crack. Such joints are known as control joints because their purpose is to control cracking. The American Concrete Institute prefers the term contraction joints because they allow for concrete contraction. Some folks call them expansion joints, but that's wrong because they don't accommodate expansion. True expansion joints are something else; we'll get to them later.

When planning a slab much bigger than 4 ft (1.2 m) in any dimension, you have three questions to answer about control joints. Will there be any? If so, how will you space them over the length and width of the slab? And last, how will you make them?

To Joint Or Not To Joint

Should you put control joints in a slab that would otherwise almost certainly crack? A yes answer might seem obvious, but cracks aren't always bad. Many indoor slabs end up covered with other materials such as carpet, tile, or wood flooring. Some outdoor slabs also get coverings. In all those cases cracks are no worse than joints. Cracks do sometimes show up through floorcoverings—but so do joints and they cause at least as much trouble when they do.

Even slabs that will be exposed to view may not need control joints if they contain enough reinforcing steel to keep cracks tightly closed. Controlling joints with steel instead of joints is mainly confined to big industrial floors and highway slabs—but the principle works on residential slabs, too, for the few inclined to try it.

The slabs that benefit most from control joints are outdoor pavements that contain little or no reinforcing steel. The typical sidewalk or driveway looks a lot better with joints than without them. In contrast, control joints don't do much in a house slab that's covered with carpet or hardwood.

Joint Spacing & Layout

Joints won't control cracking unless you space them and lay them out correctly. Follow these rules for the best results:

• If your slab is 4 in. (100 mm) thick, space the joints no more than 10 ft (3 m) apart.
• If your slab is 6 in. (150 mm) thick (or more), space the joints no more than 15 ft (4.5 m) apart.
• Keep each slab panel square or close to square. The aspect ratio—length divided by width—should not exceed 1.5.
• Avoid re-entrant corners.
• Avoid joints that form a T.
• Avoid triangular panels.

Joints give a slab a place to crack. Cast next to a big tree, this sidewalk was going to heave no matter what. But the joint looks neater than a natural crack.

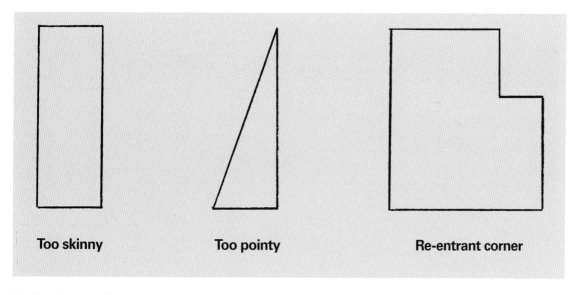

Too skinny   **Too pointy**   **Re-entrant corner**

Bad joint layout. If your joint layout results in panel shapes like these, cracks are likely.

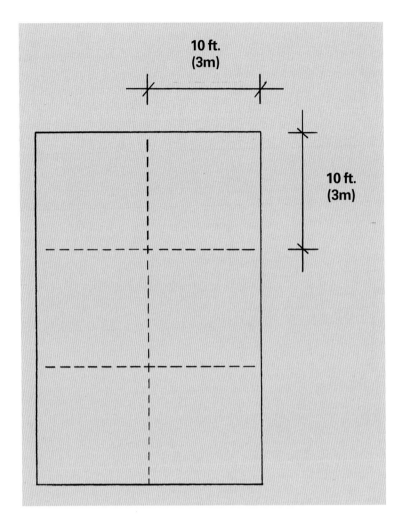

10 ft. (3m)

10 ft. (3m)

This would be a near-perfect joint layout for a slab 4 in. (100 mm) thick. All panels are square and the joint spacing does not exceed 10 ft (3 m).

The maximum joint spacings—10 ft (3 m) for slabs 4 in. (100 mm) thick, and 15 ft (4.5 m) for slabs 6 in. (150 mm) or more—are arbitrary. There is no magic spacing above which slabs crack and below which they don't. You could put joints 3 ft (1 m) apart and still get a crack. At the other extreme, some slab remain crack-free with joints over 20 ft (6 m) apart. But if you get the other details right, the recommended maximum spacings will work—most of the time.

There's one more rule that has more to do with looks than with effective crack control. The joint spacing should be uniform in each direction. Suppose you are laying a sidewalk between two driveways 31 ft apart. The sidewalk is 4 ft wide, so following the square-panel rule you start putting the joints 4 ft apart. But since 31 is not a multiple of 4, you end up with seven 4-ft panels and one 3-ft panel. That looks odd. It's better to make all the panels alike, even though none will then be a perfect square. You could divide the sidewalk into seven or eight panels, making the joint spacing either 4 ft 5 in. (31 ft divided by 7) or 3 ft 10 in. (31 ft divided by 8).

You can't always follow all the rules for joint spacing and layout. If your slab has curved sides or sides that aren't parallel, there's no way all panels can be square. If your pavement includes a re-entrant corner you can run an extra joint to it, but then you might end up with an aspect ratio above 1.5. Sometimes you just have to decide which rule to break and hope for good luck.

Ways To Make Joints

There are four ways to make a control joint:

Tool it

Saw it

Form it (turning it into a construction joint)

Install a full depth insert

All four methods have similar abilities to control cracks, but they differ greatly in appearance.

Tooled joints are made with a jointing tool. That's a small hand trowel with a ridge down the middle. You work the ridge into the wet concrete to make a groove. The groove creates a weakened plane in the concrete. If all goes well, the concrete eventually breaks directly under the groove, thereby relieving stress that would otherwise cause a random crack.

The slab cracked under this tooled control joint, just as the builder intended.

This tooled control joint did not activate. No crack formed beneath it. It is completely normal for some joints not to activate, especially in sidewalks where joints are spaced closely as much for looks as for crack control.

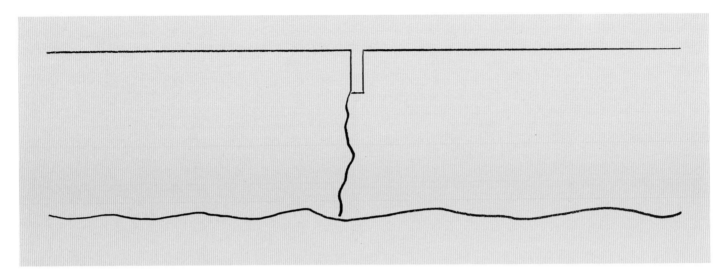

Sawn and tooled joints work by creating a notch in the slab. If all goes as planned (sometimes it doesn't) the slab cracks under the notch.

Sawn joints are made with a concrete saw after the concrete has set. They work the same as tooled joints to make a weakened plane.

Formed joints are made by stopping the pour at a side form. After the concrete has set (usually the next day), you strip the form and pour concrete on the other side of it.

Insert joints are made by pouring concrete around a vertical board. They resemble formed joints except that the board stays in place and you can pour on both sides of it at the same time. Since the insert remains visible, you need to choose a material that both looks good and lasts a long time. Treated lumber is the most common choice.

How deep do tooled and sawn joints need to go to make the slab crack beneath them? People in the concrete industry have been arguing over that for decades, and the answer still isn't clear. One commonly-followed rule says the joint's depth should be one quarter the slab thickness. That's probably a good rule for sawn joints. But it's hard to follow when you tool joints. I've never seen a jointing tool that cut more than 1 in. (25 mm) deep, and most don't go that far.

Sawn control joints

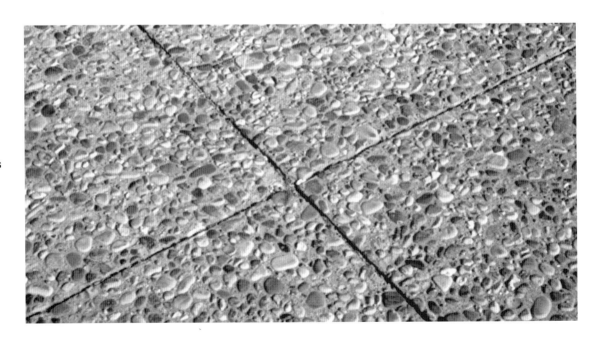

Full-depth wood insert joint

Tooled control joint

Other Kinds Of Joints

Joints do more than just control cracks. You may run into three other kinds of joints: construction joints, isolation joints, and expansion joints.

A construction joint, also known as a day joint or a formed joint, marks the line between two separate concrete pours. Since construction joints relieve stress, they often do double duty as control joints. But sometimes you need a construction just because a slab is too big to place in one day. You make a construction joint by erecting a side form and casting concrete to it.

An isolation joint separates a slab from something else. That something might be a wall, a vertical pipe, or another slab. The isolation joint includes a layer of soft material so the two sides can move slightly without interference. The material is called joint filler, or filler board, or expansion strip.

An expansion joint makes room for concrete expansion. It's made just like an isolation joint, by installing a layer of compressible material. True expansion joints are rare, because a concrete slab almost never grows bigger than its original size. Concrete shrinks as it dries, so it tends to get smaller over time. A rise in temperature will cause concrete to expand, but it would take an extreme heat wave to create enough expansion to offset drying shrinkage. Unless you pour a huge slab in cold weather, you can forget expansion joints.

Many people mistakenly say expansion joint when they mean control joint, construction joint, or isolation joint. I guess that's because some structures (though not many concrete slabs) really do need expansion joints and the name has spread.

Gradients

Indoor floor slabs are usually designed to be level, though some people slope garage floors toward the door, or basement floors toward a drain. In contrast, most outdoor slabs slope. Many of them slope because they sit on unlevel ground. But even where the ground is perfectly horizontal, slabs are deliberately tilted for drainage.

Slab slope is often described as the rise divided by the run, expressed as a percentage. If a surface goes up by 1 in. (the rise) over a horizontal distance of 20 in. (the run), the slope would be 5% (1 in./20 in.=5%). Before doing any slope calculations, make sure rise and run are both measured in the same units. It makes no difference which units you use—inches, millimetres, ancient Egyptian cubits—as long as they are the same. Americans tend to measure rise in inches and run in feet, which can get confusing. You need to multiply the run by 12 to convert it to inches. If you work in the metric system you are less likely to get into trouble, but even then you might find the rise expressed in millimetres (or centimetres, in some countries) and the run in metres, so you could still have some converting to do.

You will sometimes see floor or pavement slope expressed as a ratio rather than a percentage. A 5% slope would be 1:20. A 2% slope would be 1:50. If you are used to thinking about angles in degrees, it may help to know that a 5% slope is 2.9 degrees from horizontal.

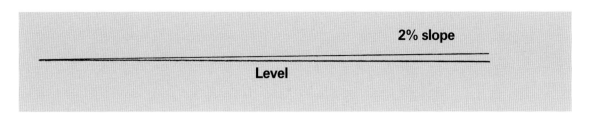

2% slope

Level

A slab surface should slope by at least 2% if you want it to shed water. A 3% slope is safer.

The traditional rule says you need a 2% slope for free drainage, and that's the usual value specified where local regulations cover the work. A 2% slope is 1/4 in. over 1 ft., or 20 mm over 1 m. But even with a 2% slope there's some risk of ponding, so if you want your slab to shed water no matter what, you might need 2-1/2% or even more. I like 3%.

Give some thought to which way you want your slab to slope. Patios should drain away from the house. Sidewalks normally drain toward the street, but if the land around them clearly slopes the other way there's no point in fighting it.

You don't normally need slope in two directions. Recommendations and even regulations say that sidewalks and driveways should slope crosswise, but that's not the only option. If your sidewalk or driveway slopes lengthwise because you live on a steep hill, you don't need to slope it 2% from side to side. You've already got all the drainage you need.

So far we have been talking about minimum slopes for drainage. But there are maximum slopes, too. Sports surface and patios should be close to level. For them, the maximum and minimum slopes are not far apart. You want enough slope to shed water, and no more. In the case of certain sports surfaces, even the minimum gradient needed for drainage may be too much.

Sidewalks and driveways generally follow the lay of the land. If your street runs up a mountainside, how can the accompanying sidewalk not do the same? Still, some limits apply. Note that 2% is the maximum cross slope—not the minimum or the target—for sidewalks subject to the Americans`with Disabilities Act Accessibility Guidelines (ADAAG). ADAAG may also limit the lengthwise slope (see sidebar on page xx). Concrete driveways can slope as much as 24%, but require special details where gradients exceed 10%.

Taking Off

is the process of determining how much material you need to buy. It's not really part of slab design, but I cover it here because it's something best done at your desk or at the kitchen table, not out in the field.

On every job you have to estimate the amount of concrete. On many jobs you have to take off other materials, too, such as formwork, reinforcement, and curing compound. It's especially important to get the concrete amount right, since you can hardly run down to the corner hardware store and get an extra wheelbarrow load if you run short.

Estimating Concrete Quantities

Concrete is measured by volume, usually in cubic yards or cubic metres. When people talk about a yard or a metre of concrete, it's short for a cubic yard or a cubic metre. A cubic yard is the amount of material that would fill a cube 1 yd (3 ft, or 36 in.) on each side. It's equivalent to 27 cu ft. A cubic metre is the amount of material that would fill a cube 1 m (100 cm, or 1000 mm) on each side. It's 31% bigger than a cubic yard.

To determine how much concrete you need, follow these steps:

1. Calculate the surface area of the slab in square feet or square metres. If the slab plan is a simple rectangle, just multiply the length by the width. That also works if you have a gently curving footpath or driveway, as long as the width stays the same. Just make sure you measure the length along the curve. If you have another shape, you had better think back to your school geometry lessons, or get help from someone who can. If you are good at drawing, sketch out the slab plan on quad-ruled paper, scaling it so each square on the paper represents a square foot, or 200 mm by 200 mm, or some other convenient dimension. Then count up the squares that lie within the slab's boundaries and multiply by the area each square represents.

2. Convert the slab thickness into the units you used to measure length and width. That will normally be either feet or metres. Thickness is more often measured in smaller units—inches, millimetres, or centimetres. (Though centimetres are no longer part of the standard metric system, called the Systeme International or SI, they are still widely used in some countries.) If you know the slab thickness in inches, divide by 12 to get feet. If starting with millimetres, divide 1000 to get metres. But if the thickness is in centimetres, divide by 100 to get metres. In almost every case the thickness will be a small fraction of a foot or metre.

3. Multiply the surface area (from step 2) by the slab thickness (from step 3). The result is the estimated volume of the slab, in cubic feet or cubic metres.

4. Add 10% to cover loss and measurement error. In other words, multiply the estimated volume by 1.10. Some people cut that to 5%, but they're gamblers.

5. If working in cubic feet, divide the result by 27 to get cubic yards. (1 cu yd = 27 cu ft). If working in cubic metres, just leave the answer as it stands.

You have now finished your concrete take-off—provided you plan to order read-mix. Just tell the plant how many cubic yards or cubic metres you want. But if you plan to mix your own concrete the fun has barely started.

Estimating Concrete Ingredients

To mix on site you don't order concrete. You order its dry components—cement and aggregates. You'll find that when batching concrete, two and two do not make four. They make less than three. The finished concrete is only about 2/3 as big, by volume, as the sum of the dry ingredients that go into it. The volume loss occurs because finer particles fit into the gaps between bigger ones.

You need to make sure the sum of all your dry ingredients—cement, fine aggregate, and coarse aggregate—is about 50% greater than the total volume of concrete needed to fill up the forms. But you can't just pile up materials till you have enough, because the proportions are critical.

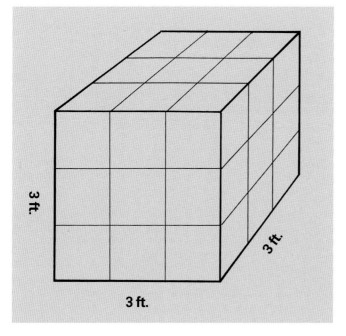

3 ft.
3 ft.
3 ft.

Concrete is measured in cubic yards or cubic metres. A cubic yard is the volume of concrete that would fill a cube 1 yard wide, 1 yard high, and 1 yard deep. It contains 27 cubic feet.

Mix proportions are written as a ratio of cement to fine aggregate to coarse aggregate. A 1:2:4 mix has one part cement, two parts fines, and four parts coarse aggregate. (That's not how ready-mix plants do it, but we're talking about site-mixed concrete now.) Once you have decided on the mix proportions, follow these steps to determine material quantities. The process is the same whether you work in cubic yards or cubic metres.

1. Multiply the concrete quantity by 1.52 or 1.56. Use 1.52 where the biggest aggregate particles are no more than 1 in. (25 mm) across. Use 1.56 where the top size exceeds 1 in. (25 mm). If you don't know the aggregate size, it's probably below 1 in. (25 mm), so you can multiply by 1.52.

2. Add up the three numbers in the mix ratio.

3. Divide each of the three numbers in turn by the sum of all three, and multiply by 100. This gives you the percentage of each component in the mix.

4. Multiply each percentage by the total volume of concrete. This gives you the amount of each component to order.

Here's an example. We'll specify a 1:2:3 mix, and assume the job will take 3.5 cu yd of concrete. The coarse aggregate is a #467 gradation with rocks up to 1-1/2 inches (40 mm) across, so we'll have to multiply the concrete volume by 1.56.

Step 1- 3.5 cu yd x 1.56 = 5.46 cu yd total dry components
Step 2- 1+2+3 = 6
Step 3- 1/6 x 100 = 16.7% cement fraction
2/6 x 100 = 33.3% fine aggregate fraction
3/6 x 100 = 50.0% coarse aggregate fraction
Step 4- 16.7% x 5.46 cu yd = 0.91 cu yd total cement needed
33.3% x 5.46 cu yd = 1.82 cu yd total fine aggregate needed
50.0% x 5.46 cu yd = 2.73 cu yd total coarse aggregate needed

Once you have the calculated the quantities in cubic yards or cubic metres, the next step is different for cement and aggregates. You buy cement by the bag, but you usually buy aggregates in bulk.

Aggregates are easy. Just call the supplier and order the cubic yards or cubic metres you need. Some suppliers sell by weight rather than volume, but that doesn't matter since they always know the conversion factors. It's better to let them do the converting, as different materials have different densities.

Cement is a bit more complicated, because it's sold by the bag.

In the United States, a standard bag of cement holds 1 cu ft. It's actually sold by weight, 94 lb, but for our purposes here it's the volume that matters. Since 1 cu yd = 27 cu ft, multiply the cement quantity (in cubic yards) by 27 to get the number of bags. Following the example started above, multiply 0.91 by 27 to get 24.6 bags. You can't buy 0.6 bag, so round up to 25 bags and you're ready to place your order.

In much of the world, cement comes in 50-kg bags that hold about 0.033 cu m. At that rate it takes about 30 bags to make a cubic metre of cement. To determine the number of bags needed, just multiply the cement quantity (in cubic metres) by 30. Please note that it's 30 bags per cubic metre of cement, not per cubic metre of concrete. The number of bags in a cubic metre of concrete will be far less and will depend on the mix proportions.

In some countries cement comes in 25-kg bags. It takes about 60 of them to make cubic metre of cement.

Estimating Bagged Concrete Mix

When mixing on site, you might choose to buy bagged concrete mix instead of separate ingredients. Cement and aggregates come already blended, waiting for you to add water. The following rules will help you determine how much bagged mix you need:

It takes about 3600 lb of bagged mix to make 1 cu yd of finished concrete.

It takes about 2100 kg of bagged mix to make 1 cu m of finished concrete.

In the United States bagged mix is sold in bags of 40, 50, 60, and 80 lb—though rarely does one store stock every size. Divide 3600 by the bag weight in pounds to get the number of bags you need per cubic yard. If you use 80-lb bags—and you should, unless your job is so small you don't need even one—you'll buy 45 bags per cubic yard.

In metric lands bagged mix is sold in bags of 20, 25, and 40 kg, and possibly other sizes. Divide 2100 by the bag weight in kilograms to get the number of bags you need per cubic metre.If you read the instructions on the bag or rely on the manufacturer's web site, you may end up with an estimate that differs a little from what you get doing it my way. If the discrepancy is just a percentage point or two, don't sweat it. The relationship between weight and volume is not that precise, anyway. But if the instructions lead you to an estimate that is 5-10% higher, find out if they are adding an allowance for loss. You already added that allowance when you calculated the volume of concrete needed. You don't have to add it twice.

Taking Off Other Materials

Estimate sub-base material just like concrete, in cubic yards or cubic metres. Indeed, if the sub-base and slab have the same thickness, as they often do, they will take the same amount of material. As with concrete, you may end up buying it by the ton, but you can still order by the cubic yard or cubic metre.

Formwork is measured in linear feet or metres.

Most other material quantities are proportional to the slab's surface area, which you calculated in step 1 when taking off the concrete. Sheet materials for curing are easy; just get enough to cover the slab's area, with a bit extra for overlapping. Curing compounds, sealers, and coating are more complex. The manufacturer will tell you how many square feet or square metres you can cover with a given amount of liquid, but the exact figure will vary with the surface texture. Slabs finished rough take more material than slabs with a smooth trowel finish. The ratio can be as high as three to one.

This builder figured carefully and ordered just enough concrete to finish the job. It is important not to run short, lest you end up with a cold joint.

CONCRETE

CHAPTER 3

Materials

Concrete flatwork takes concrete, of course, and whole books have been written just on that. It often requires other materials too: sub-bases, vapor barriers, reinforcement, products for curing, and formwork.

The Components Of Concrete

Concrete is pretty amazing stuff. You start with a pile of loose stones and sand, blend in a grey powder, and add water. In a few days this collection of cheap materials turns into a strong, solid artificial rock that can support heavy loads and last for centuries. And unlike other examples of modern industrial chemistry that take place in distant factories, concrete works its magic right before your eyes.

Ordinary concrete is made of coarse aggregate, fine aggregate, cement, and water. It may include admixtures, chemicals added in small quantities to affect the concrete's behavior.

Coarse Aggregate

This consists of rock particles more than 3/16 in. (5 mm) across. It makes up the bulk of most concrete mixes. If you tried to make concrete without coarse aggregate, you would end up with mortar or grout—a material that has some uses but shrinks too much for flatwork.

Coarse aggregate can be either natural gravel or crushed rock. Some kinds of rock work better than others, so when ordering be sure to specify that you will be using it to make concrete. Rock sold for other purposes, such as decorative landscaping gravel, may not do the job. Some coarse aggregate is sold in bags, but for the most part it comes in bulk, sold by the ton and delivered by dump truck.

For most purposes you want a blend of particle sizes from 1/4 in. (6 mm) up to 1 in. (25 mm) or even 1-1/2 in. (40 mm). The material should satisfy ASTM C 33, with a #67, #57, or #467 gradation. However, no-fines concrete calls for a single-size, unblended coarse aggregate.

Fine Aggregate

This consists of rock particles sized 3/16 in. (5 mm) and smaller. It fills the gaps in the coarse aggregate and helps give concrete a smooth surface. You can make concrete without fine aggregate, but it's a special product for special purposes. Called no-fines concrete, it has an open texture and is used in permeable pavements.

Fine aggregate is usually natural sand, but man-made sand (crushed-rock fines) replaces the natural product in some places. If you have a choice (mostly you won't), go with natural sand, and make sure you get sand suitable for concrete. You can buy fine aggregate in bulk, usually from the same people that sell coarse aggregate. You can also get it in bags, but watch out. Some of the bagged sands available in building supply houses are no good for concrete work. Blasting sand is too fine, and play sand may not have the right gradation.

This is great coarse aggregate, if you can find it. It's a crushed limestone with rocks up to 1-1/2 in. (40 mm) across.

This is more typical of the coarse aggregate found in most markets. It tops out at about 3/4 in. (20 mm).

This 3/8-in (10-mm) aggregate is too small to serve as the only coarse aggregate in a concrete slab. It is sometimes blended with coarser material, however. And it finds use in thin toppings.

Cement

Cement is the powder that, when mixed with water, forms the glue binding the coarse and fine aggregates. If you tried to make concrete without cement you would end up with a sloppy pile of wet rocks and sand.

The binder in flatwork is, almost always, Portland cement. It's made by heating limestone and clay almost to melting, and then grinding the resulting chunks after they cool. The standard product is called Type I or Type II Portland cement. Type II gains strength a little slower than Type I, but the difference is slight and you rarely get a choice between them, anyway. Chances are only one is available where you live. You might run into Type III, which gains strength faster than the other types. It can be useful in cold weather. Another variety is white Portland cement, which is similar to Types I and II but is pure white instead of grey.

Nowadays ready-mix plants often blend Portland cement with a little fly ash or blastfurnace slag. Fly ash and slag are called pozzolans and they can replace some, but never all, of the Portland cement. You don't need pozzolans to make good concrete, but if your ready-mix supplier wants to use them you might as well go along. Pozzolan-free concrete will probably cost you more.

Green Concrete?

People in the industry sometimes call concrete green after it has set but before it has cured. It's green like a fruit—unripe. New concrete is also faintly green—or greenish—in color. But what about the other kind of green, meaning less damaging to the natural environment?

The brutal truth is that concrete is far from a green building material. The making of cement requires lots of energy from fossil fuels, and releases large amounts of carbon dioxide. Concrete slabs concentrate runoff and create areas where plants cannot grow. If you want the greenest pavements you should be looking at wood chips or local stone—or no pavement at all.

If you are determined to use concrete and still want it as green as possible, here are some ideas:

- Make slabs smaller. Does the walk from the street to your front door really need to be 4 ft (1200 mm) wide? The standard single driveway may be 8 ft (2.4 m) wide, but I bet your car will fit on a 6-ft (1.8-m) slab if you have good aim. But if you're really green, what are you doing with a car anyway?
- Choose a Hollywood driveway, which consists of two concrete strips with turf between them.
- Consider no-fines concrete for outside pavements. It takes less material than normal concrete. More importantly, it lets rain pass through instead of contributing to runoff.
- Use joints instead of reinforcing steel to control cracks.
- Use the least cement that will give the results you want. Cement consumes more energy and creates more pollution than concrete's other main component.
- Replace some of the cement with fly ash or blast furnace slag. Both are industrial by-products that will be made whether you buy them or not.

Water

Water is essential to the chemical reactions that make concrete hard. Without water the cement would stay in powder form and the aggregates would remain loose.

Any water you can drink will do for making concrete. The issue with water isn't quality but quantity. Concrete mixes always contain much more water than the minimum needed for the hardening process. That extra water, sometimes called water of convenience, serves to lubricate the mix. Without it you couldn't place and finish concrete without a huge effort. But too much water weakens the finished product and increases shrinkage. Getting the water content right can be tricky, especially when you mix on site. Use too little and you'll find the concrete hard to work. Use too much and the finished product will be weak and will shrink too much.

Unfortunately you can't just measure out a precise amount of water every time, because the amount to add varies according to how wet the coarse and fine aggregates are. You have to add water in small amounts and keep an eye on its effect.

Admixtures

These are used in small quantities but can have big effects. Though you can make good concrete without admixtures, their use sometimes makes good concrete better. The admixtures you are most likely to run into are accelerators, retarders, plasticizers, and air entrainers. Some admixtures have more than one effect and cross over between those categories.

Accelerators are admixtures that make concrete set faster. They can be useful in cold weather, when normal concrete will keep you up all night. Retarders have the opposite effect, which can be desirable in hot weather. Plasticizers, also called water reducers, make concrete more workable while keeping the water content down. Air entrainers create microscopic bubbles in the cement paste. Those bubbles help concrete resist the effect of frost.

Ready-mix suppliers will gladly put any of those admixtures in your concrete. Indeed, the odds are good they will use some kind of plasticizer unless you make a point of asking them to leave it out. And in some towns all ready-mix concrete comes with an air-entraining admixture unless you insist otherwise.

Using admixtures when you mix on site is another story. I would avoid them completely in hand-mixed concrete. You just can't blend them in well enough to be sure of the results. Power mixers make admixtures more practical, but you have to take extreme care in measuring out the admixtures. Small errors in batching aggregates or cement have little effect, but getting an admixture wrong by a few ounces can cause big trouble. Remember, too, that admixture doses are usually specified in ounces per hundredweight of cement (or millilitres per 100 kilograms). When measuring admixtures it's not the amount of concrete in the batch that matters, but the amount of cement.

Buying small quantities of admixtures for mixing on site can be tricky. Manufacturers don't normally package the stuff in anything smaller than a 5-gallon (20-litre) pail. That's way too much if you are just replacing a couple of sidewalk panels. Your best source may be the local ready-mix plant. The folks there will undoubtedly have admixtures on hand and may be willing to sell you a little. It's not their core business, so ask nicely.

Where To Get Concrete

There are two ways to get fresh concrete. Either you order it from a ready-mix plant or you mix it yourself on site.

Ready-mix plants normally stock several different aggregates.

Ready-mix has powerful advantages. It's made by professionals who are used to meeting strict specifications for concrete quality. A ready-mix plant can supply almost any kind of concrete you need, including admixtures. The concrete arrives ready to go, leaving you free to concentrate on the rest of the job. And it often costs less, especially in larger quantities.

So why would anyone mix concrete on site? Well, site-mixed concrete still makes sense under some conditions. If no ready-mix plant is located nearby, you don't have a choice. If you are placing a very small slab, mixing on site will save money because ready-mix suppliers impose minimum charges.

Often the best argument for site-mixed concrete is that it lets you pour at exactly the pace you prefer. If you are short-handed, trying to get by with just one or two helpers, you may find that ready-mix puts you under too much time pressure. It's not that the truck drivers won't wait for you. They get paid by the hour and don't mind standing around. But if you take too long the supplier will charge you extra. And worse, concrete quality goes down with long wait times. You should always try to pour concrete before it is 90 minutes old, and that's 90 minutes from the time the water hits the cement, not from arrival on site. In hot weather you should keep it down to an hour. That's easy to do when you mix on site, but can be impossible with ready-mix.

Mixing On Site

Before you can start the actual mixing, you have to batch. Batching works the same way whether you mix by hand or use a power mixer.

Batching

is the process of measuring out all the ingredients. Some books say you should always batch concrete by weight, not volume. Those same books say you should always batch full bags of cement. But nobody follows those rules on small jobs. Everybody batches by volume and uses partial bags, and it usually works.

Concrete for site-mixing is specified by the ratio of cement to fine aggregate to coarse aggregate. A 1:2:3 mix has one part cement, two parts fine aggregate, and three parts coarse aggregate. A 1:2:4 mix has one part cement, two parts fine aggregate, and four parts coarse aggregate. That's what I'd use for most jobs.

The "part" in those ratios can be any unit of volume—a cubic foot, a gallon bucket, or even a container of unknown size, as long as you measure everything in the same container. The time-honored way to batch concrete is by counting out shovelfuls, but that's pretty rough. You'll get better results if you measure out each ingredient into a bucket. Overfill the bucket, smack the side to take out air pockets (especially important with cement), and strike the material off level with the container's top. Again, it doesn't really matter what size container you use, as long as you can lift it. The important thing is to measure out the cement and aggregates in the same container, or in identical containers.

A traditional choice for general purposes is 1:2:4. Changing that to 1:2:3 gives you a stronger mix that may be easier to finish because it contains more cement. On the other hand, the 1:2:3 mix costs more and shrinks more as it dries. Other ratios are possible. I like to keep each aggregate quantity a whole-number multiple of the cement quantity, but that's not essential if you can keep track of the math. Some people use a 5:14:21 mix. With that last one, you can measure everything in cubic feet (5 cu ft of cement, 14 cu ft of fines, etc.) and end up with almost exactly 1 cu yd of concrete.

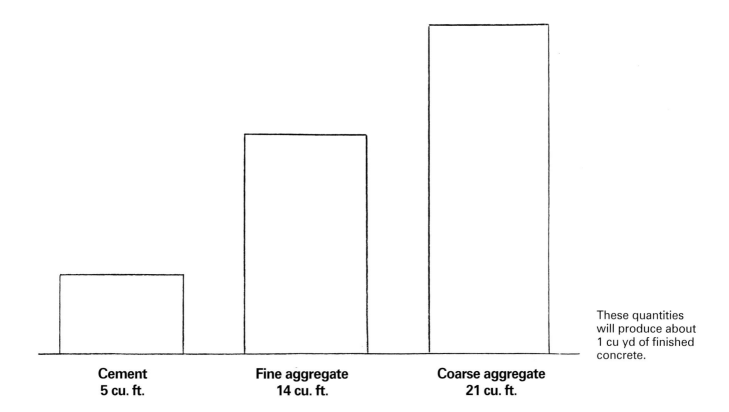

Cement
5 cu. ft.

Fine aggregate
14 cu. ft.

Coarse aggregate
21 cu. ft.

These quantities will produce about 1 cu yd of finished concrete.

You may have noticed that none of those ratios include concrete's fourth essential component, water. That's not because water doesn't matter. It matters a lot, and ounce for ounce it has more effect than cement or aggregates. The problem is that you have to account not only for the water you pour in, but for the water already present in the fine and coarse aggregates. (The cement had better be dry, always.) If you knew the exact moisture content of the aggregates, you could measure out water as you do the other components. But you don't, so you can't.

The solution is to add water slowly till the concrete has the consistence you want. Just what consistence is that, you ask? Well, it's hard to describe, but you'll figure it out soon enough. You need enough water to thoroughly wet all the dry ingredients, but not so much that the mix becomes a soupy mess. If you turn over a shovelful of wet concrete, the pile should settle but not completely flatten out, and the shape of the shovel should remain as a visible imprint. By the time you get it right you will normally have added about half as much water as you did cement, but the exact amount will vary.

After batching comes mixing. Here you have the choice between mixing by hand and using a power mixer.

Mixing By Hand

To understand concrete you should mix at least one batch by hand. You may find that one is enough.

Hand mixing is one of the toughest jobs around. And it's not just hard, but technically inferior to power mixing. Human muscles can't match a mixer when it comes to blending aggregates, cement, and water. And you can forget about entrained air when you mix by hand. The process isn't vigorous enough to work up the froth that puts air bubbles in cement paste.

If those limitations don't put you off, here is what you need to mix concrete by hand:
Cement and aggregates, piled close together

Water source, not just for mixing with the concrete but also for cleaning up

A place to do the mixing—either a sheet of plywood or hardboard laid on the ground, or a wheelbarrow, or a mortar box

Measuring container—bucket or box with lifting handles

Straight stick for striking off material in the measuring container

Square-end shovel

Once you have assembled everything you need, follow these steps:

Measure out the fine aggregate and spread it in a thin layer over the mixing area.

Measure out the cement and spread it on top of the fine aggregate.

Measure out the coarse aggregate and spread it on top of the cement.

Using the shovel, blend the aggregates and cement. Slide the shovel under all three layers, lift them, and flip them over in the center of the mixing area. Keep piling everything up in the center. When you have finished with this step, the materials should be thoroughly blended and piled high, like a miniature mountain. Make sure you mix the dry ingredients completely before you add water.

Use your shovel to form a crater at the top of the pile. Your model mountain should now look like a volcano.

Pour water into the crater. Use less than you think you will need. The first time, put in a bit less than half the volume of cement.

Continue mixing with the shovel, piling the concrete up in the center of the mixing area. Keep mixing till all the water has been absorbed and all the cement and aggregates have been wetted.

If some cement still looks dry after all the water has been absorbed, add more water. It's also OK to add water if the mix, thoroughly wetted, is just too stiff to use. But go easy. There is a fine line between just enough water and way too much, and you don't want to cross it.

If you do cross that line and end up with soup (you will, sooner or later), you can dry it up by adding more dry ingredients. But always add all the ingredients and add them in the right proportions. Don't just add cement or sand, as tempting as that may be.

You can use bagged concrete mix instead of loose aggregates and cement. That makes the job easier, but only a little. The steps remain the same, except that you don't have to measure out materials and you don't have to work quite so hard to blend the dry ingredients.

I once read a man can mix 1 cu yd (3/4 cu m) an hour. That man must work harder than I do.

Power Mixing

A powered concrete mixer beats hand mixing in every way except cost. The mixer is faster and produces more uniform concrete. It's vigorous enough to activate an air-entraining admixture, should your job call for one.

Concrete mixers come in a wide range of sizes and are available for rent. The smallest run on electricity; the rest are powered by small gasoline engines. No doubt some are better than others, but the truth is they are all good enough for small-scale slab work.

Don't trust the rated capacity of any concrete mixer. You can't fill it up, because concrete will slosh out. Generally you can mix a batch that's about one third of the total drum volume.

Here is what you need to mix concrete in a power mixer:

Concrete mixer, with plenty of fuel or extension cords, depending on the power source

Cement and aggregates (or bagged concrete mix), piled near the mixer
Water source, not just for mixing with the concrete but also for cleaning up
Measuring container—bucket or box with lifting handles
Straight stick for striking off material in the measuring container
Square-end shovel

Those are the practical essentials, but I would add a dust mask and safety glasses. The dust mask is for the dry cement that flies as you pour it into the mixer. The safety glasses are for concrete splashes when you are peering into the drum to see how the mix is doing.

Once you have everything ready, follow these steps:

Pour a small amount of water in the mixing drum. Use much less than you think you will need.

Start the mixer. Keep it turning as you add the rest of the ingredients.

Measure out the coarse and fine aggregates and put them in the mixing drum.

Measure out the cement and put it in the mixing drum.

Add most of the rest of the water. At first, before you have a clear idea how much water you will need, try an amount just under half the volume of cement.

Wait, with the mixer still running, till all the water has been absorbed.

Add more water, a little at a time, till the concrete reaches the consistence you want. Eventually you will be able to judge this by observing how the concrete slides off the sides of the mixing drum as it spins.

The general rule is that you run the mixer for one minute after all ingredients, including the last bit of water, are in. I don't see many stopwatches on construction sites, however. Most people mix till the concrete looks uniform, and then a little longer for good measure. Just remember that undermixing is worse than overmixing.

Don't forget to clean the mixer as soon as you are done. You should clean it even if you stop for lunch. Throw a shovelful of coarse aggregate in the drum, add water, and run for five minutes. Dump the contents and hose out the drum with plain water.

Ready-mix Concrete

is mixed at a concrete plant and arrives by truck. In some places you can get ready-mix concrete in a small trailer that you tow with your own vehicle. It's made by professionals who are used to meeting strict specifications for concrete quality. A good ready-mix plant can sell you almost any kind of concrete you might need, including air-entrained or colored.

How To Order Concrete

Ordering ready-mix concrete for the first time can be intimidating. Concrete suppliers are used to dealing with customers who know what they want. They are happy to take your order, but don't expect the kind of hand-holding you might get buying supplies at Home Depot or Lowe's. And bear in mind that you are not their highest priority. If you want to replace a few square feet of sidewalk on the morning the biggest contractor in town has planned a huge drydock pour at the shipyard, who do you suppose will get served first?

But don't let any of that scare you off. Just make sure you're ready when you call to place that order. You need to tell the ready-mix supplier four things:

When and where you need the concrete
The quantity of concrete in cubic yards or cubic metres
The kind of concrete (more on this below)

Ready-mix concrete is blended at the plant before delivery to your job site.

There are two ways to identify the kind of concrete you need. The easier of the two is just to say what you want the concrete for. If you say you are pouring a driveway, or a sidewalk, or a floor slab, they will send you what people in your area normally use for that purpose. The other way, which I prefer, is to specify the compressive strength in psi (pounds per square inch) or MPa (megapascals). A good choice for most purposes is 3500 psi (25 MPa). I also like to ask for a mix that contains some 1-1/2-inch (40-mm) rock in the coarse aggregate. You can't always get that, but it doesn't hurt to ask.

Don't specify ready-mix concrete by a ratio such as 1:2:4. Ratio mixes makes sense for site-mixed concrete because you can batch them with nothing more advanced than a bucket. But ready-mix plants batch by weight and have figured out exactly (to within a few pounds or kilos) how much of each component they need to achieve a given strength.

Whichever way you specify the kind of concrete, it pays to ask about entrained air. In some markets all mixes come with air unless you specify otherwise. In other markets the opposite is true. If you are laying an indoor slab with a smooth finish, you definitely don't want air. If you are laying an outdoor slab and live where freezing temperatures occur, you definitely should use air.

Always order at least one day ahead. Call again on the morning of the pour to confirm. Formwork, tools, and helpers should all be ready to go when the concrete truck pulls into sight. You'll have to be ready to pay, too; COD is the normal policy. The driver will probably take your check, and maybe even a credit card, but ask first.

Be nice to the ready-mix truck driver. He (or, far less often, she) won't expect a tip, but a friendly welcome can go a long way toward ensuring the cooperation that will make your job easier.

You will make the ready-mix driver's job easier if you have a place for washing off the chutes.

Other Materials

While the concrete gets all the glory, almost all slabs include other materials, too. Some of them are not visible in the finished product, but that doesn't mean they don't matter. Your project may involve a sub-base or vapor barrier under the concrete, reinforcement within the concrete, and a coating or sealer on top of the concrete. And every concrete pour requires formwork.

Sub-base Materials

The sub-base is the layer between the concrete slab and the ground. Not every slab gets a sub-base, but many do and more should. Unless the natural ground on your site already consists of something like gravel or sand, a sub-base will improve your slab's performance.

For most purposes the best choice is crusher-run rock. Crusher-run is the whole, unsieved output of a rock crusher. It contains a wide range of particles sizes, from 1 in. (25 mm) or so down to dust. It wouldn't make good concrete aggregate, mainly because of the dust, but it works great as a sub-base. Crusher-run compacts well, grades smooth, and holds up under foot and wheel traffic. The main drawback to is that it doesn't drain as well as some of the alternatives. If you expect rain just before you pour concrete, you may want to cover the crusher-run to keep it from getting soaked.

A sub-base made of compacted crusher-run rock. This is the ideal sub-base in every way except drainage.

Other choices include gravel and sand. Gravel is great for drainage, but you can't make it as smooth as crusher-run or sand. That means your slab's thickness will vary more. Sand is easy to place and grade, but it's equally easy to disrupt when you walk or drive on it. But I don't want to make a big deal about the drawbacks of gravel and sand. If one of them is available at the right price, use it.

The typical sub-base is 4 in. (100 mm) thick. You might want to bump that up to 6 in. (150 mm) if you are building on spongy ground.

Truth be told, a lot of contractors leave the sub-base out, even on poor soil. But that doesn't mean you should. A good sub-base, though invisible when the job is done, can make a huge difference in a slab's long-term performance.

Vapor Barriers

The most common vapor barrier is polyethylene sheet, which comes in various thicknesses. Even the thinnest poly will block most water vapor, but it's easily damaged. Try to get material that's at least 6 mils (0.15 mm) thick. Some people think the minimum thickness should be 10 mils (0.25 mm).

Recently there has been a big effort to sell special vapor barriers that are said to be better than ordinary polyethylene sheet. They probably are better, but I'm not convinced you need them except under the most severe conditions. The big dividing line isn't between various brands of vapor barrier, but between using any vapor barrier and using none at all. Even a lowly sheet of thin polyethylene can be pretty effective.

Reinforcing Steel

Not every slab needs reinforcement. If you decide that your slab does, the choices include rebar, wire mesh, and steel fibers.

Rebar—short for reinforcing bar—is steel rod with bumps on it to help grab the concrete. In the United States rebar is identified by a number that represents the bar diameter in eighths of an inch. Elsewhere bar diameters are usually given in millimetres. Rebar comes in many sizes but only two—#3 (3/8 in.) and #4 (1/2 in.) see much use in light-duty slabs. The metric equivalents are 10 mm and 12 mm.

Rebar is normally laid in a grid with the bars running in two directions. In addition to the bars themselves, you'll need tie wire to connect the bars where they cross, and something to hold the grid of bars up when you pour concrete around it. The usual

A sub-base made of coarse aggregate (not crusher-run). This drains more freely than crusher-run, but is harder to grade smooth.

supports are concrete bricks (you can make your own) or special props called chairs, made of plastic or metal. You should space the supports no more than 3 ft (1 m apart) in both directions.

Wire mesh—sticklers call it welded wire fabric—is a factory-made grid of thin wires. In the United States it's described by four numbers written like this: 6x6, W2.9xW2.9. The first two numbers give the wire spacing in inches. The last two numbers show the cross-sectional area of each wire in hundredths of a square inch. The Ws lets us know the wires are smooth; bumpy wires would get the letter D instead. The numbers come in pairs because wires run in two directions. Usually the wire spacing and size are the same in both directions, but sometimes they are not. Long, narrow slabs need more reinforcement in the long direction, and some mesh is made specially for them.

In our example the 6x6 tells us the wires are centered 6 in. (152 mm) apart, both lengthwise and crosswise. The W2.9xW2.9 in our example tell us all the wires in both directions are smooth and have a cross-sectional area of 0.029 sq in. (18.7 sq mm).

That's the official way to specify wire mesh. But many people, including some of the folks you might buy mesh from, still use an older method. They quote gauge sizes instead of wire diameters. In the gauge system a higher number means a smaller wire. The W2.9 wire from the previous paragraphs is called 6-gauge. The common W1.4 wire is also known as 10-gauge. If you ask at the local hardware store 6x6, W1.4xW1.4 mesh, you are likely to draw a blank look. If you ask for 10-gauge mesh, they will point you right to it.

Like rebar, wire mesh must be held up above the ground during the concrete pour. Concrete bricks and chairs don't work so well with mesh, however, unless you space them about 1 ft (300 mm) apart, which nobody does. Mesh sags between supports and deforms when you step on it. Some contractors pull the mesh up into the concrete with hooks, but that's next to useless. A better method is to pour the bottom half of the slab first and lay the mesh on that.

There are technical arguments about mesh versus rebar, but in practice the choice comes down to how much reinforcement you want. That's because the mesh you are likely to buy provides a tokenish amount of steel. The most common mesh size, and the only one found in many stores, is 6x6, W1.4wW1.4, often called 10-gauge or driveway mesh. When installed in a 4-in. (100-mm) slab, that mesh provides steel equal to 0.06%. In contrast, #3 rebars spaced at 24 in.—which is about as light a rebar grid

Rebar

as anyone would use—give 0.12%. That's twice as much reinforcement.

Steel fibers offer a third way to reinforce a concrete slab. Thin filaments 1 to 2 in. (25 to 50 mm) long, fibers are mixed in with the wet concrete. If you are using ready-mix concrete, you may be able to buy the steel fibers from the concrete supplier and have them added at the plant. Otherwise you can put them in the ready-mix truck when it arrives on site.

If you are mixing on site, put the fibers in last. There's no effective way to batch steel fibers by volume, so you'll need a scale to weigh them unless your mixer is so big that you can use a whole bag or box.

Dosage rates range from 25 to 70 lb per cubic yard of concrete (15 to 45 kg per cubic metre). At the lower doses fibers work like wire mesh or rebar to limit crack width. At higher doses fibers can prevent visible cracks and allow the construction of big slabs without joints.

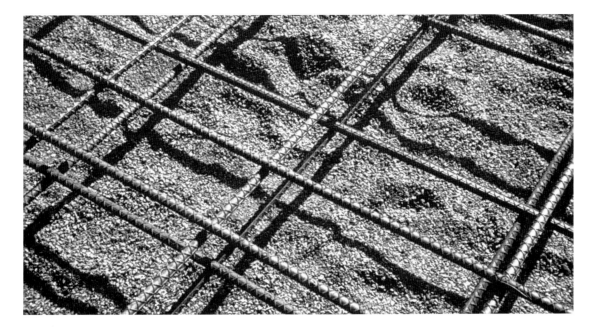

Rebar mat with bar crossings tied

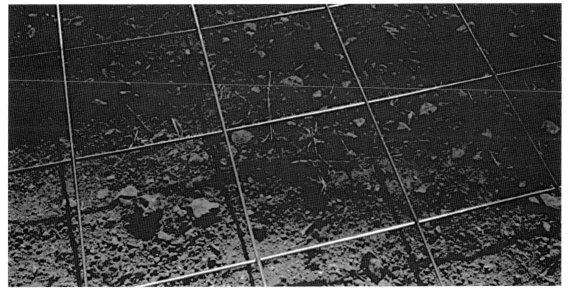

Wire mesh

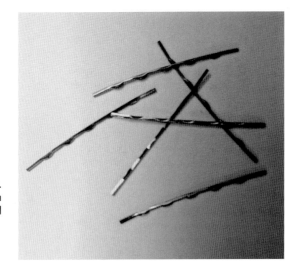

Steel fibers.
Courtesy of Fibercon
International

Steel fibers may be harder to find than rebar or wire mesh. In some areas you can buy them from your ready-mix supplier. If that's not the case where you live, or if you are mixing the concrete on site, you might have to order fibers by mail.

When asking around about steel fibers, you are likely to get a suggestion or two about using plastic fibers instead. The short answer is: don't. Plastic fibers, typically made of polypropylene or nylon, cannot effectively replace reinforcing steel.

Joint Filler

is a strip of soft material used to separate two concrete slabs, or to separate a concrete slab from something else like a wall. It's often and somewhat misleadingly called expansion strip. I say "misleadingly" because expansion isn't really the issue. Only under the most extraordinary conditions will your concrete slab ever expand to a size greater than it had the day you poured it. No, the purpose of joint filler is to allow the two sides to shift vertically without chipping or putting undue stress on the concrete.

Joint filler, suitable for isolation or expansion joints

The standard product is a brown, resin-impregnated fiber board about 3/8 in. (10 mm) or 1/2 in. (12 mm) thick. Get it in a width to match your slab thickness, and cut it to length with a knife or woodworking saw. Another option is foamed plastic joint filler, which is easier to cut and probably does a marginally better job.

Whatever you use, make sure it extends the full depth of the slab. Some contractors just cut a narrow strip and attach it to the top of the joint, letting concrete flow underneath. That defeats the joint filler's purpose.

Curing Materials

In the old days people cured concrete under piles of loose material that was kept wet. Sawdust, hay, and even manure were used. Today you have options that are, if not better, at least cleaner. The choices include absorbent sheet materials, waterproof sheet materials, and curing compounds. All can do a good job if you use them correctly.

Absorbent sheet materials include burlap and building paper. They only work if you keep them wet, so plan on hosing them down several times a day.

Waterproof sheet materials include polyethylene film and waterproof curing paper. Unlike absorbent sheet materials, they need not be kept wet. Polyethylene film, often called poly or Visqueen (a trade name), is widely used and comes in clear, white, and black versions. Any color will do indoors, or outdoors in cool weather. But if you are working outdoors in hot weather, white poly helps keep the concrete from getting too hot.

Polyethylene sheet for curing. The same material can be used as a vapor barrier under the slab.

Curing compounds work just like waterproof sheet materials, except they go on as liquids and then harden into a film. Though instructions may tell you to apply the compound by sprayer, you can always use a paint roller or brush instead. Just make sure you put on plenty. The amount you need depends on the finish; broomed or floated surfaces take more than smooth-trowelled concrete. When you are done, the surface should look completely wet with no areas left dry or speckled. If you plan to paint or seal the concrete later, make sure the curing compound is compatible with what you have in mind. If in doubt, switch to another curing method.

Sealers

are resins that coat the slab surface, like varnish on wood. A well-made concrete slab doesn't need a sealer to protect it from the elements. But not all slabs are well-made. Sealers can be useful remedies for defective surfaces. They also have their place on slabs that need protection from spilled liquids. And some people just like the look of sealed concrete.

If you buy a generic concrete sealer at the hardware store, it is likely to be an acrylic resin. Epoxy or polyurethane sealers are more durable, but also much more expensive.

Some products do double duty as curing compounds and sealers. But don't assume that any old sealer will work for curing. Certain kinds can only be applied after the concrete has thoroughly dried out, making them worthless for curing.

Formwork

Formwork makes up the mold into which concrete is poured. Elevated slabs have forms on the sides and also on the bottom. Forming elevated slabs is a complex job that lies beyond the scope of this book. Slabs on ground have forms only on the sides. The side forms define not only the slab's edges, but also its elevation.

Side forms are normally made of lumber that has a nominal width matching the slab's planned thickness. For a 4-in. (100-mm) slab, use nominal two-by-fours placed on edge. For a 6-in. (150-mm) slab, use two-by-sixes. You'll notice I said "nominal". Nowadays a so-called two-by-four isn't 2 in. by 4 in. It's only 1-1/2 in. by 3-1/2 in. You might think the missing 1/2 in. would make slabs too thin, but mostly it doesn't. That's because the target slab thickness is an average, not a minimum. If your nominal two-by-four sits on top of the highest spots in the subgrade (or sub-base should you have one), there will inevitably be lower spots too, and the average thickness will end up not far from 4 in. (100 mm).

Stakes driven into the ground hold the forms in place. Wood stakes will do, but steel ones don't split and are easier to drive into hard ground. Don't just use any old steel rods, though. Get the kind made for formwork, with nail holes drilled in them. Figure on at least one stake every 3 ft (1 m). Double-headed nails, though not essential, make it easier to take the forms down after the pour. If your form is over 8 in. (200 mm) high, you might need a few kickers—diagonal braces that keep the form from tipping over. While you probably won't pour any slabs thick enough to need kickers, the situation could arise when you cast a floor slab integrally with a building foundation. It could also come up if you need to cast a thick anchor at the low end of a steep driveway.

Steel forms can make a good alternative to lumber. They cost too much to buy for one or two jobs, but you may be able to rent them. You'll still need a few pieces of lumber around to finish the job, since you can't cut steel forms to length. (Well, I guess you could cut them if you had to, but the rental store wouldn't like it.)

Two-by lumber and regular steel forms work only for straight runs. You'll need bendy forms if your slab's edges have curves. Thin steel forms do a fine job, but as with straight steel forms the cost is too high for a single job unless you can find them for rent. The cheaper option is hardboard sawn into strips. Use lots of stakes, and fix the hardboard to them with screws, not nails.

Two-by-four lumber is the standard material for forming a 4-in. (100-mm) slab with straight sides.

Curved edges require special forms. These are steel, but you can also use hardboard.

CONCRETE

FLATWORK

CHAPTER 4

Tools

Concrete flatwork calls for some specialized tools, but with few exceptions you don't have to buy them. Most are available for rent. In this chapter we will look at the tools you may need, in the order in which you use them.

Take a good look at your tools before starting a concrete pour. Do you have everything you might need? And—just as importantly—is everything in working order and rugged enough to last the day? The last thing you need, when the ready-mix truck is on site and the clock ticking, is a trip to the hardware store to replace a broken tool, or a run to the gas station to air up the tire on your wheelbarrow.

I thought about making a checklist of tools, but that's hard because the contents of the list depend on what kind of job you are tackling, and also on your personal likes and dislikes. So you'll have to do the work. I suggest that you read this chapter with pencil and paper in hand, writing down every tool you expect to need. And if you think of something I haven't mentioned (there's bound to be something), write that down, too. Then you will have a list you can check off before the pour.

Tools For Site Preparation

The basic tool is a square-end shovel, and on many jobs you need nothing else. Depending on what sort of vegetation covers your site, you might want to rent a sod cutter. If there are big roots in the way, you'll find an axe or chain saw useful. You may need marking paint—spray paint that works upside down, to mark areas for digging.

If you have a lot of dirt to move, you'll be tempted to rent some sort of powered equipment. Before you give in to that temptation, consider the cost and how long it will take you to learn to use it effectively. This is one area where hiring a specialist contractor can greatly simplify your life.

You will usually need a level to check the grade as you go. For a small size this could be just a carpenter's bubble level. On bigger jobs you may need a laser or optical level. If you are on a low budget you can make an old-fashioned water level out of plastic tubing.

Most subgrades and sub-bases should be tamped down before you pour concrete on them. You can tamp by hand with a heavy timber or a steel plate on the end of a heavy pipe. Or you can rent a powered plate tamper or vibrating roller.

On many jobs you need a level to grade the base and set forms. An optical level like this is one option. Other options include laser and bubble levels.

Tools For Forming

You need basic woodworking tools: a claw hammer and a saw (hand or electric), and maybe a chisel if you have to notch out around an obstruction. You need those tools even if you use steel forms, because there are always a few gaps that must be filled in with wood. If using hardboard to make curved forms, add a screw gun.

Whatever your forming material, you want a sledge with a long handle for driving stakes.

Unless you are just replacing a sidewalk panel or two, you need some layout tools to help set forms at the right height. Mason's string will do the job if you are just connecting two existing pavements. Otherwise you need some kind of level. This can be a carpenter's bubble level, a laser, or a transit (optical level).

Tools For Mixing

Whether you mix by hand or in a power mixer, you need a measuring container and a square-end shovel. For power mixing, add the mixer itself and whatever you need (gas can, extension cords) to keep it running. For hand mixing, add a sheet of plywood or hardboard, or a mortar box. Alternatively you can mix on an area of asphalt or concrete pavement, but bear in mind you may have a hard time cleaning it up afterward. Some people mix concrete in wheelbarrows, but I find that awkward.

Tools For Transporting & Placing

You will probably have to transport concrete from the mixer or ready-mix truck to its final locations. And even if you can dump concrete directly between the forms, you need tools to place and level it.

Wheelbarrows & Buggies
A wheelbarrow holds about 1 cu ft (30 l) of concrete. Don't use a light-duty garden wheelbarrow for anything but the smallest jobs. Designed for light materials such as compost and mulch, it will fall apart if used for heavy-duty concrete work. Get a real contractor's wheelbarrow, even if you have to rent it.

A buggy rolls on two wheels instead of the wheelbarrow's one. It holds more concrete than a wheelbarrow—up to 7 cu ft (200 l or 0.2 cu m). Its greater capacity is a big advantage unless you have to push it uphill.

A power buggy holds still more - up to about 1 cu yd (0.8 cu m)—and offers the added benefit of an engine. It's worth a look if you have a long haul or a stiff climb.

Pumps & Conveyors
Pumps can move concrete as far as several hundred feet (over a hundred metres). The distance can be vertical as well as horizontal, making pumps a good choice for upper-story floor pours.

Unfortunately, the smaller, cheaper pumps can't handle a normal flatwork mix. They are meant for grout or pea-gravel concrete, and you can't make a good slab with that. You'll need a pump with a line diameter of at least 4 in. (100 mm). Such pumps are big and expensive and not really suited to do-it-yourself. You can, however, hire a pump with an operator if your job calls for it.

The pump you are likely to hire will have a boom—an overhead arm. The other

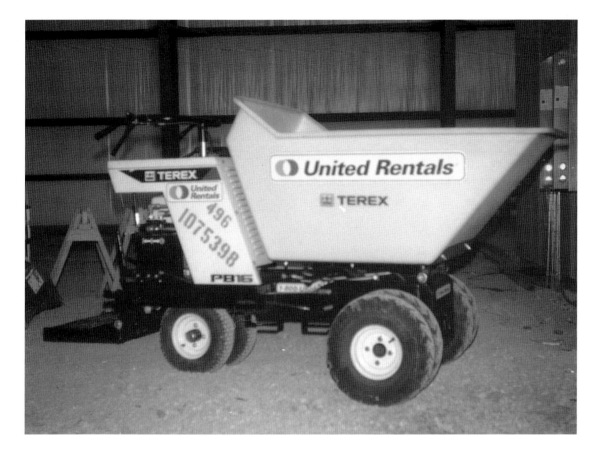

Power buggy

kind works with a pipeline assembled on site out of short sections and laid on the ground.

The pumping itself won't be your problem, but you need to get ready for it. Tell the ready-mix supplier you intend to pump. Pump mixes often differ slightly from regular concrete; your supplier will know what to do. Then ask the pump operator about priming. Concrete pumps need to be primed. The old-fashioned way is to mix up some soupy grout and run it through first. Nowadays the operator may prefer to supply a special primer that comes in a bag. If you ask first, you won't get stuck with a pump operator who's expecting a batch of grout when you have none on order. Make sure you have a place for the pump to sit, as well as room for a ready-mix truck to pull up to the hopper.

Conveyors use a moving belt to transport concrete. They can't reach as far as pumps, but on the other hand they never get clogged and they don't need priming or a special concrete mix. A conveyor may be just the ticket if you need to transport concrete a short distance over an obstacle like a garden wall or a deep ditch.

Tools For Placing

Though we talk about pouring concrete, the word pouring doesn't accurately describe the process. Normal concrete doesn't level itself out like water poured into a tank. You have to put your back into it.

A square-end shovel will do for placing, and it's what many a pro uses. But if you want a tool designed for the job, buy or rent a come-along. This looks like a rake with the tines all filled in. And you use it like a rake, pulling more than pushing. Some people use real rakes to shift concrete, but they are not the best choice because they can separate the coarse aggregate from the rest of the mix.

Modern pumps can move concrete hundreds of feet. You probably won't need one as big as this.

Once you have put the concrete more-or-less where you want it with shovel or come-along, it's time to strike it off level with the forms. The process is called screeding, and the tool for it is called a screed. Screeds are also known as rods or saw beams (because you slide them back and forth like a saw). You can buy extruded metal beams, some with handles, for use as screeds. But you will probably use the time-honored wood 2-by-4. Try to pick a straight one, and make sure it is long enough to reach all the way across your slab from form to form, with about 2 ft (600 mm) extra.

Come-along

Spreading concrete with come-alongs

These guys are striking off with an extruded aluminum beam. While that's a good choice, a straight two-by-four will also do the job.

Vibrating screed for striking-off

Consider renting a vibrating beam for striking-off. Though by no means essential, it makes a back-breaking job a lot easier, and it compacts the concrete better than you ever could with hand tools. Watch out for your formwork, however. It takes a rugged, well-staked side form to support a heavy vibrating screed. If using curved

forms made of hardboard, you had better stick with a hand screed.

As you place concrete, you should also tamp or compact it to remove air pockets. There are tools for that purpose: poker vibrators, grate tampers, and grate rollers. But you don't really need them on a 4-in. (100-mm) slab made with highly workable concrete. Most people just tamp the concrete with a shovel, come-along, or screed. Pervious concrete calls for special treatment, and is compacted with a heavy roller.

Tools For Finishing

We can classify most finishing tools as either floats or trowels (brooms are the big exception). Floats are used earlier and mostly lie flat on the concrete surface. Trowels are used later and are tilted.

Bull Floats

The bull float is basically a flat board with a long handle. Nowadays the board is usually metal, and the handle may have an adjustable knuckle that lets you tilt the board by twisting the shaft.

Bull float

Bull float with handle attached

The bull float is usually the first finishing tool to hit the slab. Its purpose is to flatten the surface, push down the coarse aggregate, and leave a workable paste on top for the next step.

Hand Floats

The original hand float consisted of a wood block with a handle. The wood version is still around, but nowadays floats are also made of plastic and magnesium. The choice of material is said to affect the surface texture of the finished slab, but I can't tell the difference. What all floats have in common is rounded or turned-up edged, in contrast to the sharp-edged trowels. Floats are always held level, with the face of the blade in full contact with the concrete.

Hand Trowels

The basic trowel consists of a rectangular sheet of steel with a handle. Unlike floats, trowels have sharp edges and are always tilted in use so that one edge drags across the concrete.

The trowels used for concrete finishing come in various lengths. I was taught to start with the longest blade and gradually work down to the shortest as the concrete hardens. But I wonder how important that is. Plenty of finishers work with just one trowel size, and power trowels always use the same blade length throughout the process. But if your budget will stretch to a full set of trowels, knock yourself out.

Don't try to finish concrete with a pointed masons's trowel. I saw someone do that once, and the results were not pretty.

Hand trowels with plastic blades are sometimes used on colored concrete to reduce marking. You won't get as smooth as finish, though.

Power Trowels

These are rotary machines that resemble upside-down helicopters. (They are even called helicopters in some languages, but that never caught on in the English-speaking world.) They can largely replace hand tools for both floating and trowelling. Higher productivity is the main reason to use power trowels, but not the only reason. Power trowelling can make a concrete surface smoother and denser than any amount

Hand floats

Hand trowel. Unlike a float, the trowel has sharp edges and is always used at an angle to the slab surface.

of hand trowelling. Power trowels are essential if you want the smoothest, so-called burnished, finish.

Steering a power trowel is like riding a bicycle: hard to analyze and describe, but surprisingly easy to do once you get over a few early mistakes. Don't shove it around like a lawn mower. Instead let the engine do the work, with you guiding it through the long handle. Raising and lowering the handle moves the machine left and right. Twisting the handle moves the machine back and forth. You may have a dark vision of the machine charging across the slab like a runaway bull, but that won't happen if you remember the kill switch. That's the lever on the handle that controls the clutch. Release that handle and the machine will stop in its tracks, giving you time to get your bearings.

Any good power trowel has controls that adjust the speed of rotation and the angle of the blades. Some cheap machines lack one or both adjustments. That severely limits their effectiveness, especially if you are aiming for a smooth trowel finish.

Various finishing attachments fit on the rotor. Float shoes curve up on both the leading and trailing edges. They are always held level and are used only for floating. Trowel blades, also called finish blades, are just flat pieces of sheet steel with sharp edges. They are always tilted and are used only for trowelling. Combination blades turn up on the leading edge and are sharp on the trailing edge. You can run them flat for floating, and tilted for finishing. Another option, good only for floating, is the disk or pan that covers the whole rotor. All those attachment have traditionally been made

Small power trowel. Called an edging trowel, this can be your main finishing tool on a small slab.

Standard-size power trowel. You can float or trowel with this, depending on which blades you mount.

Double-rotor power trowel

of steel. But non-metallic versions exist and are supposed to be better for colored concrete.

Power trowels come in several rotor diameters, the most common of which are 36 and 46 in. (910 and 1170 mm). The smaller is easier to use, and big enough for almost any residential job.

Other Finishing Tools

The derby is a long wood float with an off-center handle. It's used early in the game, at about the same time as the bull float. On wide slabs some finishers use a derby along the edges and work the middle with a bull float. Others just use a short length of 2-by-4. On narrow slabs like sidewalks a derby can relace the bullfloat altogether.

Edgers and jointers often come in matched sets, so the tooled edges and tooled joints will look similar. The edger is a small trowel with one side of the blade turned down. Its purpose is to give the slab a neat, rounded edge. The jointer is a small trowel with a fin down the middle. The fin creates a groove—the joint—in wet concrete.

The fresno is a steel trowel with a long, pivoting handle. It lets you trowel the middle of a wide slab without using kneeboards. I don't see it much these days, probably because so many people now use power trowels to finish wide slabs.

Finishing brooms don't look much different from wide pushbrooms, but they typically take the same kind of handle used on a bull float. Indeed you can probably get by with one handle for both.

The highway straightedge, also called a bump cutter, consists of a metal beam attached to a bull-float handle. When used early in the finishing process, it can replace the bull float. When used later, it serves as a scraper to take down high spots, making the slab flatter.

Clockwise From Top:
Jointing tool

Edging tool

Finishing broom

Highway straightedge, here being used to scrape down high spots

If your slab is much wider than a sidewalk and you plan to float it and trowel it by hand (no power trowel), you need something that lets you kneel on the soft concrete without damaging it. The elegant way is to use a pair of knee boards, which are like short skis that support your knees at one end and your toes at the other. They differ from knee pads, which are strapped to your knees and serve to protect you, not the concrete. Plywood will also work, if not quite so efficiently.

Other tools

A few basic tools should always be within reach, even though they don't figure directly in working the concrete. You should have:

- A utility knife for opening bags and cutting joint filler, and for all the other tasks you never think of in advance
- A few mechanic's tools (at least a screwdriver and pliers) in case you need to tighten a handle or adjust something mechanical
- A tape measure, both for layout and to figure concrete quantities

If your site lacks a water supply, you can usually borrow the ready-mix truck's hose for a little clean-up.

Concrete grinder with 10-in. (250-mm) diamond disk

If you are near a pressurized water supply, a hose will simplify cleanup. Failing that, you can usually steal a little water from the ready-mix truck, which will have a pressurized tank and a short hose.

Your need for other tools will vary from job to job. Certain specialized techniques require special tools. While this is not a complete list, you might need:
• A garden sprayer for cleaning cement off exposed aggregate, or for applying a curing compound
• Patterned mats for a stamped finish
• A graduated measuring cup for admixtures
• A heavy pipe roller for exposed aggregate or pervious concrete
• A paint roller for curing compound or sealer
• A concrete saw for making joints
• A concrete grinder for repairs

CONCRETE

CHAPTER 5

Construction Techniques

In this chapter we'll go through the steps of building a concrete slab. We'll take them more or less in chronological order, but bear in mind some of them overlap. If you're mixing concrete on site, you don't mix it all and then pour it all. You mix a little, pour a little, then mix a little more, and so on. Likewise, you can't always place all the concrete before you have to start finishing it. On a big pour someone may have to go back to the start and start floating the surface while the rest of the crew is still putting concrete on the ground.

These are the basic steps:

1. Prepare the site
2. Set forms
3. Install rebar or wire mesh (optional)
4. Mix concrete or have it delivered
5. Transport and place concrete
6. Strike concrete off level with forms
7. Finish concrete
8. Cure concrete

Site Preparation

This can be the hardest part of the project, but it's not one to skimp on. Poor site preparation can doom a slab, no matter how much effort and money you put into the rest of the process. Follow these steps:

1. Lay out the slab location on the ground. Marking paint—spray paint in a special can that works upside-down—is a good tool for this. Mark all lines about 6 in. (150 mm) outside the future slab boundaries, to leave room for the side forms.
2. Remove all turf and organic-rich topsoil within the marked lines. Don't throw it away, though. You'll need some to backfill around the slab at the end of the job, and what you don't need there can probably be put to good use elsewhere on your property. A shovel is the normal tool for this task, but you might want to rent a sod-cutter if the job is big or the grass tough. It's not unusual to find big roots—though this depends on the site, of course—so you might need a saw or ax to get them out of the way. Even if you plan to bring in fill because the site is low, you still need to dig out the turf and topsoil.
3. Grade the dirt. Your target is the planned surface elevation of the slab, minus the slab thickness and minus the thickness of the sub-base, if any. You may have to dig or fill, or some of each. If your design does not include a sub-base, take special care since the surface you grade now will form the bottom of the concrete slab. If a sub-base will go under the slab, you can be a little more casual at this stage.
4. Compact the dirt. Always a good idea, this is especially important if you brought in fill material. You can do it by hand by pounding with a heavy timber. Or if that doesn't sound like fun you can rent a plate compactor.
5. Place the sub-base, if your slab gets one. Compact it and grade it.
6. Install the vapor barrier, if your slab gets one.

A good slab needs a good base. This sub-base is made of compacted crusher-run rock.

That may all seem straightforward, but step 3—the grading—can be a challenge. We can easily say the subgrade needs to be, for example, 8 in. (200 mm) below the finish slab elevation, but where exactly is that? The slab itself doesn't exist yet. You have to picture where it will go and how much it will slope. Often there is an anchor point or two—an existing slab you have to meet, or a curb, or a doorway. Sometimes a stringline between anchor points is all you need. Often, though, it works better to rough-in the subgrade, and then fine-tune it after you have set the side forms.

Water creates a different challenge, and too much is worse than too little. While you can pour concrete on many different kinds of soil, mud is never a good choice. If it's been raining every day for two weeks and the site is heavy on clay or silt, there may be nothing to do but wait for a dry spell. If you have your subgrade ready to go and black clouds are rolling in, try covering it with polyethylene sheets to keep it dry.

Setting Forms

Unless your slab abuts an older slab, it will need forms on all sides. The forms serve two purposes: they define the slab edges, and they set the elevation for the slab surface.

For straight runs of formwork, stretch mason's twine between stakes to establish the location of the form's top edge. On many jobs you will need some kind of level to get the elevation right. This can be a bubble level on a long board, or a laser, or a transit—whichever you have and are most comfortable using. If a rectangular slab will be horizontal in one direction and sloped in the other, set one of the horizontal forms first. Then set the other horizontal form, checking its elevation against the first and keeping it higher or lower by the right amount. After that the remaining two forms are easy to set. Just run them in a straight line connecting the first two.

Curved forms are harder, because you can't bend a stringline. You will need to keep checking with the level as you go.

Anchor the forms with stakes. Do I need to mention that the stakes go on the outside of the form? You don't have to drive the stakes down flush with the forms, but the job will go more smoothly if you do.

Two-by-four side forms suffice for most small-scale slabs.

Tall side forms need kickers to keep them from tipping over when loaded with concrete.

Transporting Concrete On Site

The less you have to move concrete, the better. When mixing on site, set up your mixing area as close as possible to the concrete's final location. When using ready-mix concrete, try to arrange the job so the truck discharges its load right where you need it. The chutes can reach out about 15 feet (4.5 m), so if you can get the truck within that distance of your destination you're in luck. The benefits of pouring straight from the ready-mix truck are so great, it's worthwhile to expend some effort to make it possible. Taking down a section of fence is less work than pushing a truckload of concrete in wheelbarrows.

Rear-discharge concrete truck. If your ready-mix supplier runs this type, you'll need to take more care in arranging access.

Front-discharge concrete truck. If you have a choice, ask for this type. It has a longer chute and makes it easier for the driver to put the concrete exactly where you need it.

Often, though, you have to transport concrete on site. People in some poor countries carry it in buckets, but you don't want to do that if you can help it. That leaves wheelbarrows, buggies, and power buggies.

Wheelbarrows are popular, but don't overlook their limitations. One wheelbarrow holds about 1 cu ft (30 l) of concrete. That's not a lot. It means you have to make about 27 trips to shift a cubic yard of concrete, or 33 trips for a cubic metre. Maybe you need more than one wheelbarrow.

A buggy holds several times as much as a wheelbarrow. That's great, but only if the ground is smooth and close to level. You can't push a loaded buggy up a steep grade.

A power buggy is even bigger than the non-motorized kind, and can go uphill with ease. But of course it costs more.

Another option is pumping. Concrete pumps can shift move concrete over obstacles such as fences and garden walls. You can even pump uphill or to a building's upper stories. However, the high cost of the equipment prevents its use on most small jobs.

You might be able to find a small pump for rent. However, the more normal practice would be to hire a pump contractor who will run the equipment and put the concrete where you need it.

Once the concrete is on the ground (or on the deck, if you're building a suspended slab), spread it with a shovel or come-along. You shouldn't have to move it far at this stage.

The next step is to compact the concrete—wiggling or shaking it to remove air pockets that would weaken it. The use of a mechanical vibrator is the most effective method of compaction. But cruder methods also work on the highly workable mixes commonly used in small-scale slabs. Some people tamp the concrete with the shovels or come-alongs they use for spreading. Others rely on the screed they use for striking-off.

Life is good when you can discharge concrete directly from the truck into its final position.

Pumping concrete

Spreading concrete with a come-along

This concrete was just tamped with the flat side of a come-along.

Striking-off

You can't effectively level concrete with a shovel or come-along. For that you need a long, straight beam called a `screed. Using that beam is called striking-off or screeding.

Try to get a strike-off beam longer than your slab's width, so that the forms on both sides can support it as you saw it back and forth. Professional concrete finishers often place wide slabs with screeds that don't reach all the way across, a practice called wet-screeding. But that's hard to get right.

Striking-off with a hand straightedge

Finishing

is the process of smoothing the wet concrete and giving it the texture you want. The exact steps vary with the kind of finish. The choices include:

Broom finish
Float finish
Trowel finish
Exposed aggregate finish
Stamped patterns

One rule applies across the board no matter what finish you choose. Do no finishing while bleed water is present on the slab's surface. Bleed water is free liquid that rises to the top of the slab and collects there. Concrete bleeds because water is lighter than any other ingredient. The heavier components tend to settle, leaving water to bleed out the top. The amount of bleed water depends on the subgrade or sub-base (dry ground absorbs sucks some moisture from the concrete), on the concrete mix, on slab thickness (thick slabs bleed more), and on weather. Some slabs produce no visible bleed water at all.

Bleed water isn't harmful unless you make the mistake of mixing it back into the slab surface with your finishing tools. Then you end up with a weak surface that may flake off.

To prevent that harm, wait till all bleed water has evaporated before you start any finishing operations. Sometimes—usually when the weather is cold and damp—bleed water seems to take forever to evaporate. It's permissible then to slide the bleed water off the slab with a straight board or a rubber hose.

With bleed water the issue is too much water at the slab surface. You can also have the opposite condition—a surface that dries out because of wind or low humidity, or because you waited too long to get on it. When that happens you will be tempted to sprinkle water on the slab. Some people say you should never yield to that temptation, but I'm not one of them. A little extra moisture to replace what evaporated does no harm, and is sometimes necessary for a decent finish. If you expect extreme drying conditions, prepare for them either by protecting the slab with a windbreak or misting it with a fine water spray.

Broom Finish

This is common on sidewalks and driveways, where it gives good traction. It's rarely used on interior floors, which usually get a smoother finish. I don't think it's the best choice for patios, because it's too rough for some folks' bare feet. Though some might disagree, I believe a broom finish is easier for beginners to get right than its chief rival, the float finish.

From Left:
Bull-floating

More bull-floating

With a mix like this, you can use the bull float almost immediately after placing concrete. But with some mixes you have to wait.

Broom finish

To broom-finish a slab, follow these steps:
1. After striking off, wait for bleed water to evaporate.
2. Smooth the surface with a bull float. Overlap passes by about 2 in. (50 mm).
3. Gently drag a finishing broom across the surface. Either push or pull the broom as you prefer, but pick one or the other. Sweep all the way across in one motion, without stopping. Don't overlap passes. Wipe the brush clean after each pass.

You have a choice whether to tool edges and joints before or after you broom. If you tool first, you can then broom over everything to give the slab a uniform look all the way across. But if you broom first, the tooling will create a frame of smoother concrete all the way each slab panel. I prefer the framed look, but it's up to you.

This slab was broomed to the edge.

This slab was broomed first and then edged.

A variant called the scratch finish is sometimes used on slabs that will be covered with toppings or thick-set ceramic tile. A wire brush replaces the soft finishing broom.

Float Finish

This is widely used on sidewalks, driveways, patios, and sports surfaces. It's also used on some indoor slabs --mainly those that will get floorcoverings such as tile or carpet. A float finish is largely interchangeable with a broom finish but is slightly smoother.

To float-finish a slab, follow these steps:
1. After striking off, wait for bleed water to evaporate.
2. Smooth the surface with a bull float. Overlap passes by about 2 in. (50 mm).
3. Wait for the concrete to firm up. When it's ready for floating, you should able to stand on the concrete and leave an impression about 1/4 in. (6 mm) deep.
4. Work the whole surface with a hand float. Don't tilt the float, but keep it in full contact with the concrete. Since the swirl marks made by the float may remain visible after you are done, try to follow a regular pattern as you sweep the float over the surface.
5. Tool the joints, if applicable.
6. Tool the edges.

Hand-floating

You can use a power trowel for step 4. Fit the power trowel with a disk, float shoes, or combination blades held level. Don't use sharp trowel blades, also known as finish blades.

Trowel Finish

This is the standard finish for indoor floors, though some get a float finish instead. It's too smooth for most outdoor slabs, and you should never use it on air-entrained concrete, indoors or out.

To trowel-finish a slab, follow these steps:

1. After striking off, wait for bleed water to evaporate.
2. Smooth the surface with a bull float. Overlap passes by about 2 in. (50 mm).
3. Wait for the concrete to firm up. When it's ready for floating, you should able to stand on the concrete and leave an impression about 1/4 in. (6 mm) deep.
4. Work the whole surface with a hand float. Don't tilt the float, but keep it in full contact with the concrete.
5. Tool the joints, if applicable.
6. Tool the edges.
7. Work the whole surface with a steel trowel, as many times as needed to produce the degree of smoothness you want. Hold the trowel almost level at first. As the concrete hardens, tilt the trowel blade more and more, and bear down harder on it. The more times you trowel the concrete (to a point), and the harder you bear down, the smoother the finished surface will be. You may have to re-tool joints and edges between trowel passes.

Power-trowelling with a double-rotor machine

A power trowel can substitute for hand tools in steps 4 and 7. For step 4, use a disk, float shoes, or combination blades held level. For step 7, use combination blades or trowel blades, tilted. Start slow with the blades almost level. Increase both speed and tilt as the concrete hardens. If you want the smoothest possible finish, called burnished, you have to use a power trowel. Hand trowelling doesn't exert enough pressure. Even with a power trowel, you can expect to do a little hand trowelling around the edges.

Power-trowelling
with a small edging
machine

Generally, when people choose a trowel finish they want it as smooth as possible. But exceptions exist. Sometimes a smooth trowel finish would be too slippery, and a float finish too rough. And if you are using white cement or colored concrete, hard trowelling can leave ugly dark marks. In those situations that answer is a flat trowel finish—so called because you keep the trowel almost parallel to the slab surface, rather than tilting it more and more as the concrete sets.

Exposed-aggregate Finish

Most finishing methods aim to hide the coarse aggregate under a paste of cement, sand, and water. An exposed-aggregate finish does the opposite, putting the stone out in the open for everyone to see. It's a popular choice for footpaths, driveways, and patios. You don't see it much indoors, and it makes no sense on any slab that will get a floorcovering.

You could simply expose the ordinary coarse aggregate found throughout the slab—and sometimes people do that. But it's more normal to seed the slab surface with special aggregate chosen for its good looks.

To give your slab a seeded, exposed aggregate finish, follow these steps:

1. Strike the concrete off low—1/4 in. (6 mm) below the top of the side forms—using a board notched at each end. The low strike-off leaves room for the aggregate you will add in step 3.
2. Wait for bleed water to evaporate.
3. Sprinkle coarse aggregate on the surface. This takes care; you want the rocks to cover the whole slab without gaps, but they should remain just one layer deep. And timing is critical. Seed too early and the aggregate will disappear into the wet concrete. Wait too long and the rocks won't sink deep enough for proper embedment.
4. Run a heavy roller over the surface to flatten and embed the aggregate. A lawn roller (you can rent one) will work, but so will any big, heavy pipe.
5. Wait. The concrete needs to get hard enough so that you don't dislodge the aggregate in step 6. But if you wait too long you won't be able to expose the aggregate fully.
6. Use a broom to sweep the paste off the top of the aggregate. The goal is to leave about one third of each stone exposed. If you expose much more than that, you increase the risk the aggregate will break loose.
7. Spray the surface with water and gently brush or wipe to remove the cement paste left behind in step 6. The key here is to spray gently so you don't dislodge aggregate or remove too much paste between aggregate particles. A garden sprayer is safer than a hose hooked up to city water.

Does all that sound hard? It can be. But that needn't stop you if you are determined to have an exposed-aggregate finish. To make success more likely, watch out for three things. First, keep the concrete mix as uniform as possible. If one batch is drier or wetter than another, they won't set at the same rate and it will be impossible to expose all the aggregate at exactly the right stage. Second, seed the aggregate evenly, covering every square inch with one layer, and no more than one layer, of stones. Third, watch the timing of steps 3, 6, and 7. You can't follow the clock, because the concrete doesn't. Just keep checking every few minutes, trying the next step on a small scale to see if the concrete is ready for it.

Pros get around the timing challenge by spraying the fresh concrete with a chemical retarder. That stops the cement on the surface from setting. Workers can then take their time exposing the aggregate. Sometimes they wait overnight.

You can use chemical retarder, too, but I don't encourage that unless you are pouring a slab that's intimidatingly big. Despite what you may hear, the retarder isn't essential and doesn't necessarily improve the results.

Stamped Patterns

are made by pressing a mat into the wet concrete. It sounds simple, but it's far from easy. You have to get the timing right, and even then it takes considerable force to put the mat in full contact with the slab surface. Some people walk on the mats; others pound them with mallets.

While in principle they could make a mat that just leaves a pretty pattern, the common mats are all designed to make concrete look like some other paving material, such as brick, cobbles, or flagstones. Because those other materials tend to have distinctive hues, stamping is often combined with some sort of color, which can take the form of an integral pigment or a stain applied later.

By now I hope you have noticed that one of this book's themes is the idea that you, an amateur or at any rate not a concrete specialist, can match professional concrete finishers when it comes to small-scale flatwork. But with stamped concrete I have to back away from that position. Truth is, even the pros often bomb when they try this. It's not that stamping is so much harder than other finishing methods. Rather it's that

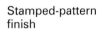

Exposed-aggregate
finish

Stamped-pattern
finish

stamping leaves no room for error. At best, a stamped finish looks something like brick or stone. But make a small mistake, either in the stamping or in the color, and you get a lousy imitation of brick or stone that will annoy you every time you look at it.

If you are still brave enough to try a stamped finish, follow the instructions that come with the mats you rent. They're not all the same. Most if not all instructions call for you to coat the mats with form oil, and that's a step you don't want to forget. Without it the mats may stick, not only ruining your work but possibly the mats as well.

Joints require special attention in stamped concrete. For one thing, the joints should, as much as possible, line up with the fake mortar lines in the stamped pattern. For another, the joints should be spaced closely to minimize the risk of random cracks. Even a narrow crack—one you might ignore in plain, float-finished concrete—can spoil the look of a stamped pavement.

Edging

is the process of smoothing and rounding the slab edges. No matter what finish you choose—except maybe exposed aggregate—tooling the edges is part of the job. You use an edger, a special trowel with one edge turned down. No other tool will do.

Even a small crack can look bad in a stamped slab.

From Left:
Working the slab edge with a hand float before using the edger

Tooling an edge

Plan on edging at these locations:
• At all side forms
• Where a new slab abuts a slab previously placed
• At expansion and isolation joints
• Where a slab meets a wall.

Timing depends on the look you are aiming for. With a broom or float finish, you can edge before or after you work the main slab surface. If you tool first, the regular finish then extends almost to the slab edge. That gives a uniform look to the slab, but you have to take care not to damaged the tooled, rounded corners with your brooming or floating. If you tool last, you end up with a band of smoother concrete framing the slab. With a trowel finish, you may have to edge several times as the concrete hardens so that the edges will match the interior.

Jointing

You can make a crack-control joint in four ways:
- Stop the pour at a side form and pour the far side later.
- Install an insert.
- Make a groove in the wet concrete with a jointing tool.
- Saw the joint after the concrete has set.

The first two methods take place before the concrete pour and are part of the forming process. The last two methods, tooling and sawing, take place after the pour and are harder to get right. When people talk about jointing a slab, they are usually referring to tooling or sawing. Both are good methods for creating crack-control joints within a slab.

Tooled edges

From Left:
Tooling a joint

Tooled joint

Tooled Joints

Tooling is cheap and fast. It's cheap because you do it with a simple hand tool instead of a power saw. It's fast because it takes place while the concrete is soft, and it does not lengthen the finishing process. In contrast, sawing involves an extra step after the concrete has been finished.

You tool joints with a special trowel called a jointer or jointing tool. A jointer often comes in a matched set with an edger, and it's good for them to match if the smooth band created by the tools will remain visible when the job is done. The jointing tool has a fin running down the middle of its blade to form a groove in wet concrete. The edger, in contrast, has a fin down one side of its blade.

Some people—and I have to raise my own hand here—think tooled joints look better than sawcuts. But more than a few people hold the opposite view, so you'll have to decide for yourself.

The depth of the fin determines the depth of the joint, and that's where tooling becomes controversial. The deepest fins stick out about 1 in. (25 mm), but many are smaller. Some only go down 3/8 in. (10 mm). Many authorities say crack-control joints should be one fourth the slab's depth. If we follow that rule, then a 1-in. (25-mm) jointer would just work in a 4-in. (100-mm) slab. A shorter fin or a thicker slab would mean inadequate joint depth.

But hold on. For years folks have been using 3/8-in. jointers on 4-in. (100-mm) slabs with good results. Sure, sometimes a 3/8-in. (10-mm) joint won't work, but you can say the same about joints that meet the one-fourth-slab-depth recommendation. It seems that the standard rule was arbitrary and not based on much science. Recent research has shown that where the slab thickness is uniform, even a very shallow groove—as little as 1/12 the slab thickness—can control cracks. And it's possible that tooled joints, because they are created while the concrete is still young, work better than sawcuts at shallow depths.

What's the last word, then, on the depth of tooled joints? I bet we haven't heard it yet. But here's my suggestion: if you still have Grandpa's old jointer with the 3/8-in. (10-mm) fin, go ahead and use it. As long as you take care grading the site and laying out the joints, you will probably do fine.

As with edging, the right time for jointing depends on the look you want. You can tool the joints either before or after you work the main slab surface. Jointing first leaves the joints less obvious, but you have to take care to keep cement paste from entering the grooves. Jointing last is simpler, but it leaves a band of smoother concrete that draws attention to the joints. You may or may not like that.

To make straight joints, lay down a board and run the jointer along it.

Sawn Joints

Sawing works with any slab finish and any slab thickness. Because it has almost no effect on the slab surface profile, it's a good choice for floors that will get vinyl tile or sheet vinyl. Tooled joints often show through such floorcoverings, but sawcuts usually don't.

You could cut one or two joints in a sidewalk using an abrasive blade in a carpenter's circular saw. Beyond that you should use a real concrete saw. There are two kinds: downcutting and upcutting. Both kinds of saws rely on circular blades drive by gasoline or electricity, but differ in the direction of spin.

A downcutting blade spins so that its leading edge is driven down into the concrete. Downcutting saws are often called wet saws because most depend on water to control dust. However, some have vacuum attachments and are meant to be used dry.

An upcutting blade spins the other way. Since upcutting tends to chip concrete, the saw includes a pressure plate—a slotted metal sheet that presses tightly against the concrete surface as the blade slices up through it. Upcutting saws are known as early-entry saws because they can be used early, while the concrete is still fairly soft. They cut dry—but if you use them early enough they don't put much dust in the air.

Always mark joints before you saw them. A plain chalkline will suffice for dry sawing, but wet sawing will wash it away. You can seal a chalkline with clear varnish in a spray can, or you can mark the line with a lumber crayon. Normally joints run square to the slab edges. But if you have broomed a slab and the broom grooves are almost but not quite square, you might want to follow them instead. It can look odd if the broom grooves are not parallel to the joint.

The standard depth for sawn joints is one fourth the slab thickness. That means a 1-in. (25-mm) cut in a 4-in, (100-mm) slab, or 1-1/2 in. (38 mm) where the slab is 6 in. (150 mm) deep.

Timing matters, and it differs between upcutting and downcutting saws. The basic rule is the same for both: saw as early as you can without damaging the slab surface. But with upcutting saws you can get on the slab a little earlier; that's their selling point. And with downcutting saws you can saw much later if you have to without creating a dust storm.

With any saw you should always try to cut a slab the day you pour it. Slabs often crack on their first night as the temperature falls. Early sawing will, with a little luck, ensure that those cracks occur where you want them. However, in cold weather you may have to wait overnight because it can take that long for the concrete to gain enough strength to take the stress of sawing.

A new sidewalk awaits the saw. Sawing always takes place after the slab is completely finished.

Curing

After you have finished the concrete and cut the joints, the slab looks done—except for the minor matter of removing the side forms and filling in where they stood. But this is no time for complacency. One key step remains: the concrete needs to be cured.

You cure concrete by keeping it moist and frost-free so the chemical reactions that make it strong can continue. If concrete dries out early or, what's worse, freezes, it won't achieve anything close to its potential strength.

A curing experiment. The area on the left is being cured under polyethylene. The area on the right is being cured with a 30%-solids acrylic curing compound. The area at the bottom is being left uncured.

This is one area where you can easily beat the professionals, because they often ignore curing completely or make only a token effort. There's no excuse for that. Good curing is cheap and easy; there may be nothing else you can do to your slab that has a higher ratio of benefit to cost.

Since freezing is only an occasional risk, the main point of curing is to maintain moisture in the concrete for several days. In years past people sometimes ponded water on slabs or covered them with wet straw, sawdust, or even manure. Today you are likely to choose one of these three methods:

Cover the slab with an absorbent fabric like burlap and wet it down often.

Cover the slab with polyethylene sheet.

Apply a chemical curing compound.

Absorbent fabric does a great job, but only if you keep it wet. In hot or windy weather you may have to hose it down several times a day.

Polyethylene sheet—some call it poly or use the trade name Visqueen—comes in clear, black, and white varieties. Any color will serve indoors, so get whichever costs least. But outdoors you have to consider the effect of sunshine. In warm weather use white poly to protect the slab from the sun's heat. Because polyethylene is slippery, especially when wet, don't use it where people would have to walk on it.

96

Poly can cause dark and light streaks on the finished slab. Though they fade eventually, they can be obvious at first.

Absorbent fabric or polyethylene should stay down for at least three days, and a week is better. You can't cure concrete too long. Every day it stays moist it gets stronger, though the daily gain diminishes over time.

Curing compounds remove the time pressure because they stay on indefinitely. However, curing compounds vary widely in their ability to slow moisture loss. The best, which typically contain about 30% solid material, are almost as effective as absorbent fabric or poly. The cheap compounds are less effective, and I won't use them on flatwork.

Whatever method you choose, start curing as soon as possible after the last finishing step.

If you expect air temperatures to fall much below freezing, your curing method should include insulation. You can rent special blankets for this purpose. Since the blankets stop moisture loss as well as heat loss, they can replace whatever you would have used for curing in mild weather. If you can't get your hands on special blankets, any loose, fluffy material spread over the slab may save the day. Straw, leaves, and sawdust have all been used to keep concrete from freezing.

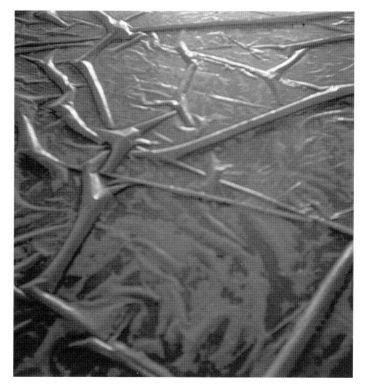

Curing under polyethylene sheet. The wrinkles can cause temporary streaks on the finished concrete surface.

Colored Concrete

Some of us think plain gray concrete looks just fine. But if you want to color it, there are three ways: integral pigments, colored dry shakes, and stains. Bear in mind that some colors work better than others. Browns and dark reds usually turn out OK. If you want bright yellow or blue, you may be disappointed.

Integral pigments are colored powders that are mixed with the wet concrete. You can order them from your ready-mix supplier, who will send the concrete out with the pigments already blended in. The price is high because it takes a lot of pigment to produce a noticeable effect, and you need to use it throughout the mix even though only a bit of it is visible on the slab surface. Because the whole slab is colored from top to bottom, chips and scratches are less noticeable than with other methods.

Colored dry shakes are pigmented aggregates blended with dry cement. You sprinkle them on the slab surface while it is still soft and work them in with a float. The cement in the shake absorbs water from the concrete below it and becomes part of the slab. That's the idea, anyway. Dry shakes are hard to get right and even experienced contractors sometimes struggle with them. Never put a dry shake on air-entrained concrete. The air gets trapped under the shake and causes the surface to peel off.

Stains are colored liquids that go on after the concrete has hardened. Like woodworking stains, they penetrate some areas better than others. That means the color may not turn out as uniform as you would like. Don't apply a curing compound to a slab that will be stained, because the compound may keep the stain from soaking in as it should.

I recommend caution when considering any form of colored concrete. The risk of failure is high, even for experienced builders.

Paint

I won't tell you never to paint a concrete slab. No, on second thought I will tell you just that. Unlike wood and metal, concrete doesn't need paint to protect it from the elements. The only reason to paint it is to make it look good, and it will look good only as long as the paint stays intact. Sooner or later—and it's always sooner than you had hoped—the paint will flake off or wear off, and then the concrete will look worse than if you had left it bare.

If you cannot abide the look of plain concrete, try covering it with something durable. Ceramic tile, stone, or brick pavers may do the job. Unlike paint, they will probably last as long as you do.

When colored concrete goes wrong, the result can be far worse than if you had left it plain.

Painted concrete usually looks great at first. It doesn't always stay that way.

CHAPTER 6

Projects

In this chapter we will look in more detail at some flatwork projects: footpaths, driveways, patios, sports surfaces, and interior floors.

Sidewalks & Footpaths

Every sidewalk is a footpath, but not every footpath is a sidewalk. Sidewalks fall in the public right of way. For that reason they are subject to rules that control their location, width, gradient, materials, and sometimes other details. You may own the sidewalk and the land under it, but your local government will have a say in how you build it. If other sidewalks on your street are made of brick or stone, you probably won't be allowed to use concrete at all.

Dimensions

In most American towns, sidewalks in residential neighborhoods are 4 ft (1200 mm) wide and 4 in. (100 mm) thick. But don't take my word for it. Call downtown and find out. Some places require 5 ft (1500 mm) of width, and a few towns want 5 in. (125 mm) of thickness. The rules may specify the distance between sidewalk and curb, but this often varies from neighborhood to neighborhood. You can usually curve or narrow a sidewalk to avoid taking out a tree, but that's about all the latitude you'll get in laying it out.

Footpaths located away from the public right of way aren't subject to any of those restrictions. You can let your imagination run wild. Private footpaths can be straight or curved, narrow or wide, utilitarian or decorative.

Make footpaths 4 in. (100 mm) thick, unless the local code requires more. Some people make them thicker—6 in. (150 mm) where they cross driveways. That probably makes sense if the driveway slab itself is that thick, but most aren't.

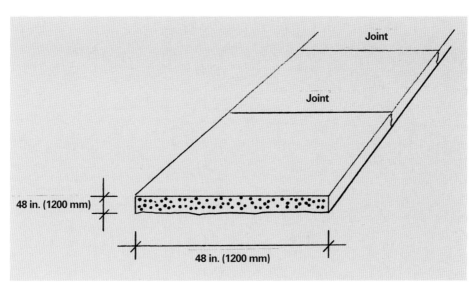

Sidewalks are usually basic concrete slabs, but private footpaths can be as fancy as you care to make them. This one has an exposed-aggregate finish.

The typical American sidewalk

Joint

Joint

48 in. (1200 mm)

48 in. (1200 mm)

Gradients

Slope the path 2% to 3% from side to side for drainage, unless the lengthwise slope exceeds 2%. Then you can make it level from side to side. But if you are laying a sidewalk subject to ADAAG, keep the cross slope under 2%. Some authorities say sidewalks should slope toward the street, but I'd deviate from that if the land slopes the other way and you have bare ground between the pavement and the street.

Longitudinal slope normally follows the lay of the land. But slopes above 8% can be hard for some people to navigate, especially if snow and ice occur where you live. Consider adding a step or two and keeping the slabs closer to horizontal.

Concrete

Normal-strength concrete is all you need for any footpath. Ask for 3500 psi (25 MPa) unless the local code says otherwise. Use air-entrained concrete unless the temperature never falls below freezing where you live.

No-fines concrete can be a good choice, especially if you want to minimize water runoff.

The ADAAG Minefield

If you are building a sidewalk in the United States, it may have to meet the American Disabilities Act Accessibility Guidelines (ADAAG). These rules are designed so that disabled people, including those relying on wheelchairs, walkers, and crutches, can use public rights of way. While that's a worthy goal, meeting (or even understanding) the guidelines can be tough.

The rules call for a 2% maximum cross slope. There's a problem, since 2% is the minimum slope needed for a free-draining surface. How can you meet minimum and maximum values that are the same number? You can't, so something will have to give.

Fortunately ADAAG allows lengthwise slopes to exceed 2%—but by how much? Interpretations vary. One rule requires handrails on ramps with more than 5% slope. Is a sidewalk that follows the road grade considered a ramp needing rails if its slope exceed 5%? Answers vary. Some local governments say yes and limit ordinary sidewalks to 5%. Others let it go up to 8%. And some hold that any slope is acceptable as long as it matches the roadway's. Road gradients sometimes exceed 15%.

ADAAG calls for a ramp down to street level wherever a sidewalk reaches a crosswalk (whether marked or not). You probably won't have to worry about this unless you have a corner lot. Obviously the ramp will slope, but its slope should not exceed 8.3%.

ADAAG does not apply to private footpaths such as those leading to a house's front door.

Joints

Footpaths seldom contain reinforcing steel. In its place they rely on closely spaced transverse joints to control cracks. The joints divide the pavement into panels that are square or nearly square. In other word, the distance between joints is about equal to the path's width.

In addition to their main job of controlling cracks, the joints are the dominant visual features in most footpaths—so it pays to get them right. A path looks better if all panels are the same size. To accomplish that, divide the path length by its width and round off to a whole number. Then divide the path length by that rounded-off number. The answer is the distance between joints.

Joints can be tooled or sawcut. Tooling gives a more traditional look. Some footpaths—but very few sidewalks—have decorative wood strips for joints.

Many builders install isolation joints where footpaths abut building walls or other pavements. An isolation joint consists of a layer of relatively soft material that prevents direct contact across the joint. Ask for "expansion joint material" at the building supply store. It's usually 3/8 or 1/2 in. (10 or 12 mm) thick. You don't necessarily have to use isolation joints. But if you do, make sure they reach all the way from the top to the bottom of the footpath slab. Some people just put a narrow strip of material at the top of the joint, resulting in something that looks like an isolation joint but does no good at all.

Decorative footpath with exposed-aggregate finish and wood-insert joints

An unusually wide footpath may need a control joint down the middle.

Finish

The traditional American sidewalk gets a float finish with tooled edges and tooled joints. The slab is floated first, and then the edges and joints are tooled. The result is a kind of frame a couple of inches wide around each slab panel. The frame is smoother than the rest of the panel because of the effect of the edging and jointing tools.

In recent years, however, more and more people are giving footpaths a broom finish from edge to edge. To achieve that, tool the edges and joints before applying the broom. Always broom parallel to the joints (that is, at right angles to the footpath edges) and use a light tough to avoid messing up the slab and joint edges.

While most footpaths get either a float or boom finish, other options exist. You can use an exposed-aggregate finish or a stamped pattern. The only finish you should not consider is a smooth trowel finish. It would leave the concrete too slippery.

Driveways

Driveways differ in important ways from most other flatwork around the house. They have to support heavier loads—cars and trucks instead of people and furniture. They may have to climb steep grades. And they have to meet other pavements—typically a public road at one end and a garage or carport floor at the other.

Dimensions

Single driveways are typically at least 8 ft (2.4 m) wide, though you can get by with less. There is no upper limit to width, as long as you can bear the expense and your local government allows that much impervious surface. But if the slab is over 10 ft (3 m) wide, you should add one or more longitudinal joints to control cracking.

Driveway length is whatever it needs to be, with transverse joints to control cracking.

Most driveways are 4 in. (100 mm) thick. Some codes call for 6 in. (150 mm), and you might consider that thickness even where not required if the driveway will have to support heavy trucks. Highway slabs are sometimes 12 in. (300 mm) thick or more, but you'll never need anything like that. Highways are thick because they have to resist fatigue caused by high-speed truck traffic. Even if big trucks sometimes use your driveway, the stresses won't approach those found on a main road.

Gradients

If your site is level, slope the driveway at least 2% from side to side so it will shed water.

If your site is not level, you will probably have to slope the driveway from end to end. Gradients up to 24% are possible, but slopes above 10% require special attention.

A driveway sloped above 10% can slide downhill. A more-or-less horizontal pavement at the bottom of the slope will stop the sliding. If there's no room for that, anchor the tilted slab by thickening it at the low end.

Where the slope exceeds 12%, cars could bottom out when going from the driveway into the road, garage, or carport. To prevent that, give your pavement a lazy-S profile, as shown below. The transition areas should be at least 12 ft (3.6 m) long. The transitions make the slope in between even steeper, but that's a price you have to pay to stop cars scraping.

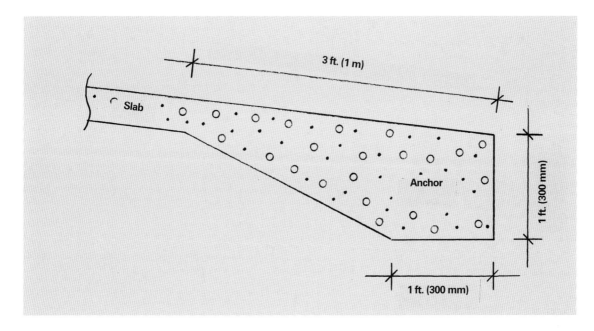

If a driveway's slope exceeds 10%, an anchor like this at the low end will keep the slab from sliding downhill.

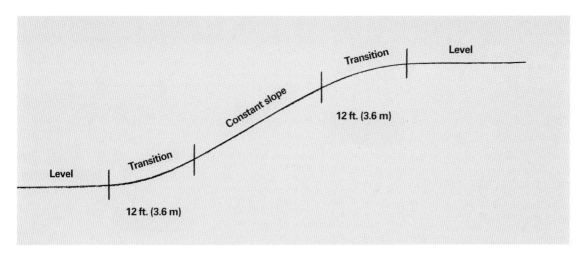

A very steep driveway needs transition curves to keep cars from scraping.

105

Concrete

Normal-strength concrete works fine on driveways. Ask for 3500 psi (25 MPa) unless the local code says otherwise. Use entrained air if you live where freezing temperatures occur.

Since driveways are larger than most other slabs around the house, it's a good idea to do what you can to control the concrete's drying shrinkage. If you can find it, use coarse aggregate with some 1-1/2-in. (40-mm) stone in it. If your supplier works with ASTM C 33 gradations, ask for #467 instead of #57 or #67. Keep the cement content down to what's needed for strength. Keep the water content down to what you need for reasonably easy placing and finishing.

No-fines concrete can be a good choice, especially if you want to minimize water runoff.

Joints

These are important both to control cracks and to give visual interest to what would otherwise be a blank expanse of plain concrete. Single driveways generally get joints in one direction only, across their width. Double and wider driveways need joints in two directions. All the standard rules for joint layout apply. Keep the panels close to square and avoid re-entrant corners. Joint spacing should not exceed 10 ft (3 m) if the slab is 100 mm (4 in.) thick. You can ease that to 15 ft (4.5 m) in 6-in. (150-mm) slabs.

Any method of jointing—tooling, sawing, or the use of full-depth inserts—will work in a 4-in. (100-mm) slab. But avoid tooled joints in thicker slabs. The tooling may not go deep enough to ensure a crack under the groove. Sawing and inserts work at any slab thickness.

Some people caulk driveway joints, but most don't. The benefits of caulk are negligible under most conditions.

In addition to the control joints within the slab, you may need an isolation joint where the driveway buts up against a sidewalk, building, garage floor, or carport floor. Use filler board, also called expansion strip, at least 3/8 in. (10 mm) thick. Make sure it reaches the full depth of the slab.

Finish

Never put a smooth trowel finish on any driveway. It will leave the surface too slippery, and if the mix contains entrained air the surface could scale off.

If a driveway's slope exceeds 10%, it's best to give it a broom finish for skid resistance. If the slope goes above 14%, you might even go to a scratch finish—similar to but coarser than a normal broom finish.

Apart from those limitations, almost any kind of concrete finish is suitable for a driveway. While most concrete drives are either floated or broomed, your finish options also include exposed aggregate and stamped patterns. If you're ambitious you can try colored concrete.

Hollywood Driveways

Before covering half your yard with a concrete slab, consider the Hollywood driveway. It consists of two narrow strips to support your car's tires. Though some might consider it old-fashioned, the Hollywood driveway has a lot to recommend it. It uses far less concrete than a full driveway and has minimal effect on water runoff. It takes twice the formwork labor, and that may explain why it's not popular with contractors. But that needn't deter you. And it's the perfect choice if you are working alone or with a single helper.

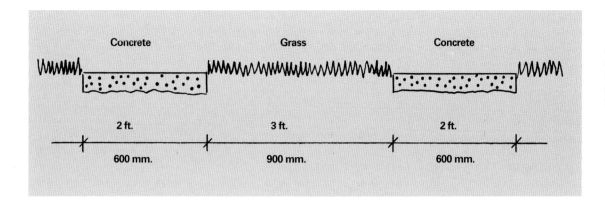

Concrete	Grass	Concrete
2 ft.	3 ft.	2 ft.
600 mm.	900 mm.	600 mm.

A Hollywood driveway consists of two parallel strips to support the car's tires.

Patios

Patios differ from most other exterior slabs in that you spend a lot of time on them. For that reason looks and comfort are important considerations.

Mixed paving looks good on a patio.

Dimensions

Patios come in all sizes, but here's a starting point. Patio tables in the United States are commonly round and 48 in. (1200 mm) across. A table that size needs a slab at least 12x12 ft (3.6x3.6 m) to give room for chairs and space to walk behind them. A cozy table for two can fit on a patio 6x6 ft (1.8x1.8 m), which would take only a quarter as much concrete as the bigger one. If you entertain big groups, consider several small patios instead of one giant.

Regardless of length and width, 4 in. (100 mm) is a good thickness for almost any patio slab.

Gradients

Slope your patio by about 2% so it will shed water. You don't want much more than 2% if you plan to put furniture on it. That means you may have some heavy grading if you live on a mountainside. If you have to build up dirt on the low side to get a level base, be sure to spread it out beyond the edge of the patio and compact it well.

Patios that butt up to the house should always slope away from the house. Elsewhere the slope should follow the natural lay of the land.

Concrete

A standard 3500-psi (25-MPa) mix will do fine for any normal patio. If your patio is more than 10 ft (3 m) long, you might try to get coarse aggregate with a 1-1/2-in. (40-mm) top size to reduce drying shrinkage, but it's no big deal if you can't.

Use entrained air if you live where freezing temperatures occur.

Joints

If the patio stretches over 10 ft (3 m) in any direction, use joints to break it up into two or more smaller panels. Joint spacing should follow the standard rules.

Since joints have a big effect on a patio's appearance, give some thought to just what effect you want. Sawcut joints and plain formed joints look utilitarian. Unless that's the look you are going for, choose tooled joints or wood inserts instead.

Sports Surfaces

Concrete slabs make good platforms for many sports. Basketball, tennis, and shuffleboard are all commonly played in backyards on concrete courts. A sports slab is a lot like a patio, but there are a few special points to keep in mind.

Dimensions

The size of the pavement matters, but more for some sports than for others. A tennis court needs to be sized just right so the foul lines will be the proper distance from the net. Basketball players, in contrast, seem able to tolerate some variation.

The table below lists standard slab sizes for several sports:

Sport	Dimensions in feet	Dimensions in metres
Basketball (NBA)	94x50	28.7x15.2
Basketball (high school)	84x50	25.6x15.2
Basketball (junior high)	74x42	22.6x12.8
Basketball (minimal half court)	30x25	9.1x7.6
Pickleball	60x26	8.3x7.9
Shuffleboard	52x10	16.0x3.0
Tennis	114x56	34.7x17.1
Volleyball	60x30	18.3x9.1

If you need a court for any other sport, you can probably get court dimensions from the sport's governing authority. Note that many games require a buffer zone around the legal area of play. If that buffer zones needs to be paved, your slab will have to be bigger than the official court size. In some sports the buffer can be turf.

A slab thickness of 4 in. (100 mm) will suffice for almost any sport surface.

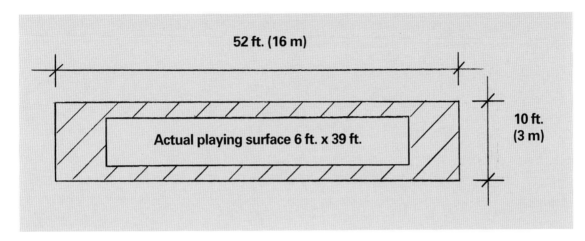

52 ft. (16 m)

Actual playing surface 6 ft. x 39 ft.

10 ft. (3 m)

The slab often needs to be bigger than the official playing surface. This is a shuffleboard court.

Gradients & Drainage

Drainage can be tricky on sports surfaces. You want the slab to drain so you can play after rain without splashing through puddles. But the usual way to ensure drainage—sloping the slab surface—affects play. For positive drainage a pavement should slope by at least 2%, and 3% is safer. In contrast, some authorities recommend a maximum 1.5% slope for basketball and shuffleboard courts. And tennis can be even stricter; I've seen recommendations for a 1% maximum slope, and also for 0.56%, which is so close to level you might as well not bother.

One way to resolve the dilemma is to place a level slab using pervious concrete, which lets rainwater go right through. But first make sure the pebbly texture of pervious concrete will work with your sport. It's been used successfully for tennis and basketball.

Another option is finish the slab level and keep a squeegee handy so you can push the water off after a rain.

Joints

Decide whether you can accept joints crossing the area of play. If you can, follow the standard rules for slab jointing. Sawn joints effect the slab's flatness a little less than do tooled joints.

If you can't live with joints, add reinforcing steel and let it crack.

What if you don't want joints or cracks? Consider post-tensioning, which has been used on some tennis courts. If done with care, post-tensioning can give you an unbroken slab with no joints or cracks.

Post-tensioning offers the possibility of a joint-free, crack-free sports surface.

Finish

The general rule is that indoor flatwork gets a smooth trowel finish, while outdoor flatwork gets a rougher finish, usually broomed or floated. That rule doesn't apply to outdoor sports surfaces. Some of them need a smooth finish for the quality of play.

If you play where freezing weather never comes, the need for a smooth finish won't cause you the slightest trouble. Trowel the slab till it's as smooth as you want. If, on the other hand, you live in snow country, you face a dilemma. Your slab should have entrained air to resist freeze-thaw damage. But if you put a trowel finish on air-entrained concrete, it is liable to delaminate.

Any solution involves a compromise. You can use air-entrained concrete and finish it with a light touch. Or you can leave the air out and apply a sealer, hoping it keeps out enough moisture to prevent frost damage.

Interior Floors

Interior floors differ from exterior slabs in more than their location. They usually get a smoother finish, and they often need protection from subgrade moisture. They may be tied to footings that support other parts of the building. They often end up covered by other materials—floorcoverings such as carpet, wood strips, tile, or vinyl.

Because they form part of a building, floors are often subject to code requirements that don't apply to outdoor pavements. The building code may impose rules on subfloor insulation, vapor barriers, and termite protection.

Under The Floor

Many floor slabs are laid over vapor barriers, thermal insulation, or both. Your local building code may require them. Even if it doesn't, they may be wise additions if the floor is located in an inhabited space—that is, inside your house. They do less good in garages and sheds.

A vapor barrier reduces the flow of water vapor barrier from the ground into the concrete slab. Water vapor doesn't harm concrete. But a wet slab transfers moisture into whatever material lies on top of it, and that's where the problems start. Many floorcoverings can be damaged by moisture. And even those that are immune are sometimes stuck down with moisture-sensitive glues. Moisture rising through the slab can also contribute to mold and mildew growth.

The usual vapor barrier consists of polyethylene sheet. Any thickness of poly will slow the transmission of vapor, but for good performance and durability some authorities recommend material that's 10 mils (0.25 mm) thick. The barrier usually goes right below the concrete, but it can also go under the sub-base, if your floor has one. Putting the vapor barrier under the sub-base may reduce slab curl, but it's not a big deal. If you're using subfloor insulation, the vapor barrier should go under the insulation.

Floors in heated buildings are sometimes insulated. If you are hoping to save on heating and cooling bills, note that the floor is the least effective part of the building envelope to insulate. Insulation does far more good in roofs and walls. Still, insulation under the floor has some value in reducing heat loss, and it makes a slab more comfortable under foot. It's especially useful when combined with an in-floor heating system.

Insulation is usually confined to the building's perimeter, in a band extending about 5 ft (1.5 m) in from the edge. It takes the form of rigid foam boards, firm enough to walk on. Don't even think of using the soft insulation found in walls. The concrete's weight would crush it to almost nothing, rendering it useless.

For best effect, insulation should form a continuous layer—a so-called thermal break—from underneath the slab up into the wall. The presence of a concrete foundation wall complicates that. So does the need for termite protection—if that applies where you live. The easiest way to provide the thermal break it to turn the sub-slab insulation up at the wall, keeping it between wall and slab. But that leaves insulation exposed at the floor surface, which may complicate the installation of floorcoverings. One alternative is to notch the foundation wall so the vertical insulation is just hidden under the interior wall finish. Another alternative is to bevel the top of the vertical insulation so the concrete covering it tapers to nothing at the extreme edge.

Insulation under the slab should not reduce the slab thickness. That means you have to dig out the subgrade or sub-base to make room for the insulation boards.

Dimensions

Length and width are dictated by building and room dimensions.

Thickness is normally 4 in. (100 mm), but some building designs call for thicker sections under walls. If the slab is part of the building's foundation, you will normally tie it to footings around the building edge and under any bearing walls. Whether you call that a thickened edge or a slab tied to a footing becomes a matter of semantics. Either way, you need a tall side form to contain the concrete. The form may need kickers to keep from tipping over when you place concrete against it.

Where possible, I prefer to support the building frame on its own footings and keep the floor slab independent of them, with isolation joints between slab and walls. Slabs and walls both settle over time, but usually at different rates. Tying them together forces them to settle together. That causes stress and, eventually, cracks.

Gradients

Unlike outdoor pavements that are sloped to shed water, most floors should be as level as you can make them. The only common exceptions to that rule occur in basements, which are known for getting wet and where you might want water to flow to a floor drain or sump pump. If that applies to your floor, aim for a 3% slope. Some say the slope should be 2%, but unless your finishing skills are well above par, aiming for 2% will leave birdbaths.

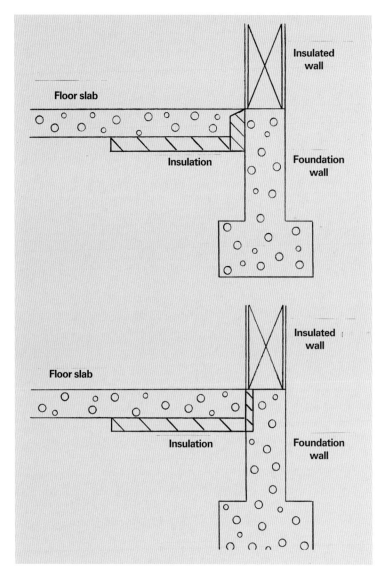

Sub-slab insulation (where used) should come up between slab and foundation wall to provide a complete thermal break. Here are two ways to accomplish that without leaving insulation exposed at the slab surface.

Concrete

The concrete strength to ask for depends on the floor usage. If the concrete will be exposed and will form the wearing surface, as in a garage or unfinished basement, use concrete with a 28-day compressive strength of 3500 psi (25 MPa). But if you plan to install a floorcovering, reduce that to 3000 psi. The lower-strength mix will cost less and shrink a little less. It may be slightly harder to finish because of its lower cement content, but that won't matter if you are going to cover it up.

Don't use entrained air—even if you live in a cold climate, and even if the floor lies in an unheated room. The concrete will probably never freeze while soaking wet, as an outdoor slab might, so you needn't fear frost damage.

Joints

Crack-control joints matter less in floors than in outdoor slabs, because in most floors the cracks and joints will be hidden by floorcoverings. If the concrete will be hidden from view, I'd argue that jointing is a waste of time and money. Just let it crack.

If you don't buy my argument, or if the slab will be exposed and you care about its appearance, follow the standard jointing rules. Any jointing method will work fine in an exposed slab. But if the slab is going to be covered with vinyl tile or sheet vinyl, sawn joints will probably look better than tooled ones.

Whatever you decide to about crack-control joints within the slab, you may need isolation joints where the floor meets other building elements. Use filler board, also called expansion strip, at least 3/8 in. (10 mm) thick. Make sure it reaches the full depth of the slab.

Finish

Floors normally get a smooth trowel finish. It's easy to clean and works with any kind of floorcovering. However, if you know beyond doubt that a slab will get thick-set tile or some other flooring that's laid in mortar bed, there's no harm in leaving it rough.

If you want to apply a curing compound, make sure it won't interfere with any coating or glue that will go on later. Curing under wet absorbent materials or polyethylene sheet is always safe because it leaves no residue to interfere with anything.

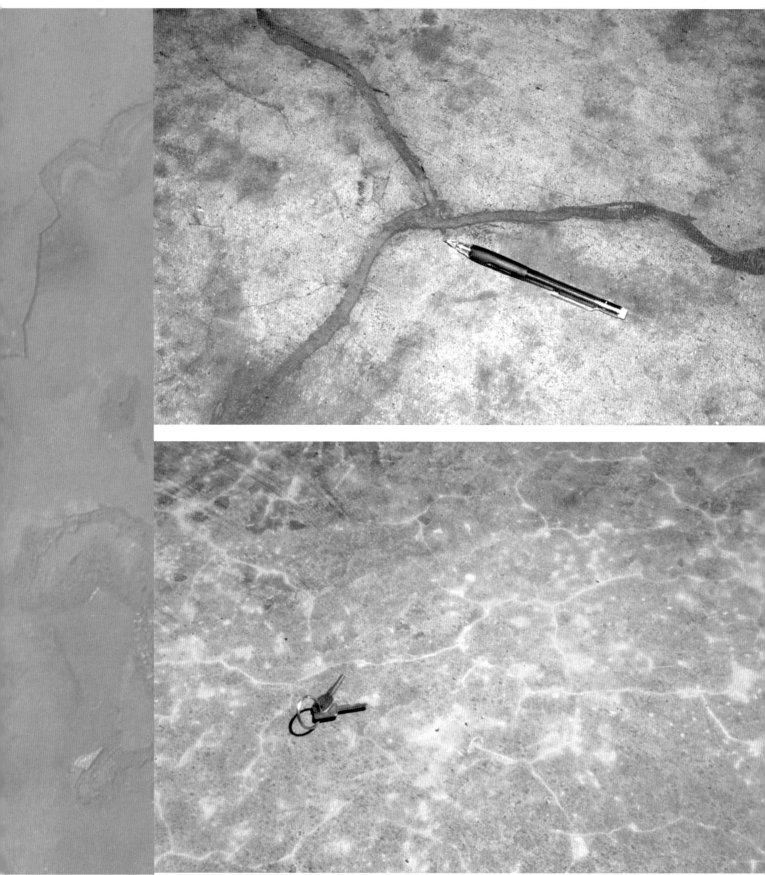

CHAPTER 7

Problems & Repairs

Many things can go wrong in concrete flatwork, both during construction and afterward. In this chapter we will look at some and consider how to prevent them or fix them.

Problems During Construction

These can include cold joints, concrete that sets too fast or too slow, and bad weather.

Cold Joints

A cold joint occurs when fresh concrete is placed next to concrete that has begun to set. It normally results from a delay in the pour, but something similar can occur when the concrete mix changes during a pour. Cold joints rarely cause real structural damage. But they look bad because you can never get the finishes to match across the joint.

Cold joint

To reduce the risk of and damage from cold joints, follow these rules:
- Avoid long delays in the concrete pour. If you are mixing on site, that means no lunch break and no running out of materials. If you are buying ready-mix concrete, it means ordering enough so you don't have to wait for a small make-up load at the end.
- Keep the concrete mix as consistent as possible from batch to batch.
- If a delay occurs despite your best efforts, rake down the old concrete to form a ramp. That will create a transition zone between the old and new batches. The transition will reduce the visual effect of the cold joint.

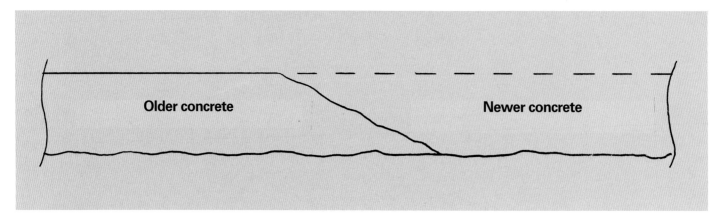

Older concrete   Newer concrete

Try to avoid long breaks during a concrete pour. If one occurs anyway, rake down the older concrete to make a tapered transition zone.

Slow Setting

Sometimes concrete is slow to set because it has been mis-batched or contaminated, but that's rare. Most slow setting is the result of cold weather. The chemical reactions that make concrete hard are affected by temperature. Heat speeds the reactions up. Cold slows them down.

Patience is often the best solution. Provided it stays above freezing, cold weather won't hurt concrete. If you wait long enough the concrete will set and you can finish the job.

If you hate waiting, try one of these steps to speed things up:
- Heat the mixing water.
- Add a chemical accelerator to the concrete mix. The cheapest accelerator is calcium chloride, but you shouldn't use it in reinforced slabs outdoors because it promotes corrosion of the reinforcing steel. Chloride-free accelerators are available but they cost more.
- Use more cement in the concrete mix.

On indoor pours you may be able to heat the room you are working in.

Fast Setting

Concrete sets faster in hot weather. This is a bigger problem than slow setting in cold weather, because you can always work slower but you can't always work faster. If the concrete hardens before you can finish it properly, you will not have a good day. You could even lose the whole slab.

Try one of these steps to slow the setting rate:
- Pour at night or early in the morning.
- Replace some or all of the mixing water with ice. Ready-mix plants will add ice, for a fee.
- Add a chemical retarder to the concrete mix.
- Use less cement in the concrete mix.
- Replace some of the cement with fly ash or blastfurnace slag.

Weather

The perfect day for concrete work would have moderate temperatures, overcast skies, fairly high humidity, no rain, and no wind. In the real world a day like that comes about once a year, so you learn to compromise. Many a good slab has been laid in questionable weather. On the other hand, some conditions can ruin your job.

Rain is what everybody fears when placing concrete outdoors, but it's seldom as bad as it looks. A sprinkle or drizzle does little harm, and may even make your job easier by keeping the concrete from drying too fast. Even heavier rain generally won't ruin concrete if it falls early in the day. But if it comes when you are ready to finish, all bets are off. Sometimes you can save a slab from a downpour by covering it with tarps or polyethylene sheets (which you may have on hand for curing, anyway). If the rain goes on, you may have to pull the covers off, work the slab surface briefly, then cover it again. You might even have to repeat those steps several times. If rain gets the better of you, it need not mean the end of your slab. The damage usually remains skin-deep, and you can repair it by grinding.

High wind can be worse than rain. It dries the slab surface, causing craze cracks and plastic-shrinkage cracks. In the worst cases the concrete crusts over while it's still soft underneath, ruining the finish. The best defense against high wind, as with rain, is to wait for better conditions. People rarely cancel a pour for high wind, but they should. Two other ways to fight wind are to erect a windbreak (seldom practical, but effective if you can pull it off) and to spray an anti-evaporative film on the concrete between finishing steps.

Freezing

Freezing can damage a slab it two ways, depending on the concrete's age when the temperature falls. Freezing during the first day or two of a slab's life can totally ruin it. Ice crystal forming throughout the concrete destroy its fabric, rendering it useless. The only way to prevent early freezing is to protect the new slab from dangerous cold. Once damage has occurred, there is no fix short of removing and replacing the affected concrete.

The risk changes after a few days. One cold night will no longer cause total destruction. The danger now comes from repeated cycles of freezing and thawing while the concrete is saturated with water. The damage shows up as spalls at the floor surface. In mild cases the slab surface just looks pockmarked. In bad cases the whole surface disintegrates. You can prevent, or at least greatly reduce, freeze-thaw damage by using air-entrained concrete. The air-entraining admixture puts microscopic bubbles in the cement paste. Those bubbles give water a place to expand into as it freezes, relieving the pressure that causes surface popouts.

Repairing Defects

You can't prevent every defect. Fortunately, few flatwork defects are so serious that the slab must be replaced. Some defects are best ignored, while other can be repaired without too much trouble.

Repair Principles

There's an old Navy saying that goes, "Do something, even if it's wrong." On the other hand, Hippocrates told doctors, "First, do no harm." When it comes to fixing floor defects, I have to side with Hippocrates. Take your time figuring things out, and try not to make them worse. Sometimes the best repair is no repair at all.

Repairs on top of repairs. A little thought and caution might have prevented this.

Two rules apply to almost all kinds of slab repairs:

- Make the repair no bigger than absolutely necessary to eliminate the defect. If a crack is 1/16 in. (1.5 mm) wide, don't go routing out a groove 1/2 in. (12 mm) wide just so you can fit some caulk into it.
- Never patch to a feather edge. Cut back to a vertical edge at least 1/2 in. (12 mm) high. If you want a truly flush repair, overfill the hole and grind or sand it down after the patch material has hardened.

This sidewalk had faulted joints, so someone replaced slab panels here and there. Grinding would have cost less and looked better.

Cracks

Whenever lay people talk about defects in concrete slabs, cracks are a main topic. When a driveway or sidewalk cracks, people worry. They fear that something has gone seriously wrong and needs to be fixed. That's understandable, because in everyday life cracks tend to be undesirable or even unacceptable. If you get a crack in your coffee mug, or your car's windshield, or your computer screen, you'll want to do something about it.

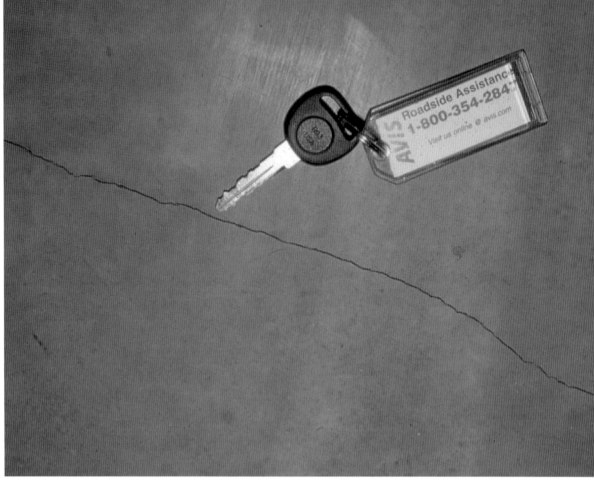

Would a crack like this keep you awake at night? If so, maybe concrete flatwork is not for you.

But concrete is different. Almost every slab above a certain minimum size is broken up into smaller pieces to accommodate drying shrinkage and temperature changes. Sometimes we deliberately create the smaller pieces, and then we call the breaks joints. Other times the concrete breaks up on its own, and then we call the breaks cracks. Joints and cracks look different but function the same. A joint is just a planned crack, and a crack is, most of the time, just an unplanned joint. When you look at cracks that way, they become less alarming.

When faced with a crack, start by asking whether it needs repair at all. Most don't. The cracks you need to worry about meet one or more of these conditions:
* The crack has faulted leaving one side noticeably higher than the other.
* The crack has rough, chipped edges.
* The crack is so close to a slab edge, joint, or another crack that a chunk of concrete is likely to break out between the crack and the other feature.

For faulted cracks, the standard fix is to grind down the high side. That's straightforward, but it changes the appearance of the slab surface. If your slab has a decorative surface such as exposed aggregate or a stamped pattern, you won't be happy with the results of grinding. The alternative is to inject grout under the low side, but that requires special equipment and usually costs more.

For other crack problems, the remedy normally consists of some sort of filling. Many different crack fillers are available, and it can be hard to match the product to the problem. If the crack is functioning as a joint, opening and closing in response to concrete shrinkage and expansion, you need to fill it with something elastic so the slabs can keep moving. But if the crack was caused by an event that probably won't recur, you can use a strong, hard glue and lock the slabs up. If the crack is less than 1/8 in. (3 mm) wide you will be hard pressed to get anything into it other than an expensive, low-viscosity polymer resin. But if the crack's that narrow, why are you repairing it in the first place?

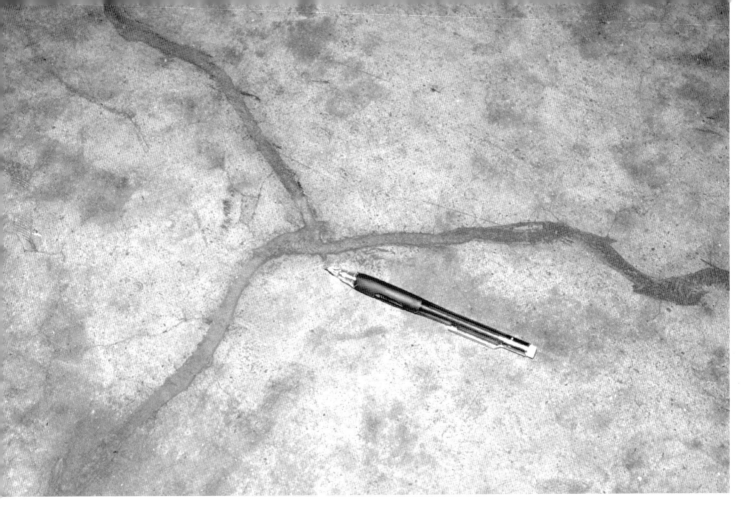

Someone put a lot of effort into repairing these cracks, and the results look good. But to make room for the crack filler the original hairline cracks had to be routed out. Leaving them alone might have been a wiser move.

While many cracks don't need repair, we can probably all agree that this one does.

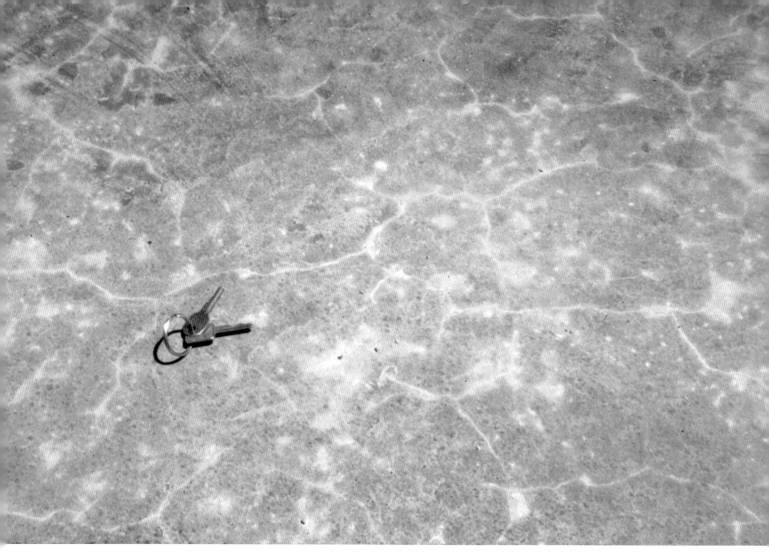

Narrow craze-cracks like these are usually harmless.

Popouts & Potholes

A popout is a small chip in the slab surface. The usual cause is an impurity—a wood chip or a piece of defective aggregate—in the concrete mix. A pothole is wider and may be caused by frost or a pocket of weak concrete. You can repair both the same way:

1. Cut into the slab just outside the damaged area on all sides. Make a vertical cut at least 1/2 in. (12 mm) deep. You can make the cuts with hammer and chisel, but a core drill (for popouts) or a concrete saw (for potholes) works better.
2. Chip out the concrete inside the cuts, at least 1/2 in. (12 mm) deep.
3. Vacuum up all dust and debris.
4. Moisten the bottom of the repair area—but only if you are using a cement-based patch material. Leave it dry if using epoxy.
5. Mix up a patching mortar, following the instructions on the bag or can. While it's possible to whip up your own mortar, this is one case where I recommend buying a manufactured product design for patching concrete. Some rely on cement and are mixed with water. Others are based on epoxy and come in two cans that you must blend together.
6. Fill the hole with the patching mortar.
7. Finish the mortar to match the surrounding concrete, as best you can. It won't be perfect. If the surrounding concrete has a smooth trowelled finish, leave the mortar high and grind it down after it has hardened.
8. If using a cement-based mortar, cure it by keeping it moist for at least a couple of days. Epoxy doesn't need curing.

Delamination sometimes starts like this, as blisters that pop up as you trowel the concrete. Other times it comes without warning.

Delamination

Delamination occurs when the slab surface peels away from the underlying concrete. It's often related to entrained air. Ironically, air's presence and absence can both lead to delamination, under different conditions. The presence of entrained air causes delamination when someone puts a smooth trowel finish over it. The lack of entrained air contributes to delamination when concrete is exposed to freeze-thaw cycles while wet. Mistakes in finishing can also cause delamination, with or without entrained air.

To prevent delamination—or perhaps I should say to reduce the risk of it—never put a smooth trowel finish on air-entrained concrete, and always use entrained air in outdoor concrete that will be exposed to freezing weather.

To repair delamination, treat small, isolated examples as you would popouts or potholes. If the delamination is too widespread for that—and it often is—you have two options: grinding and topping. Whichever you choose, start by chipping off anything that you can easily loosen. A hammer will do the job, but on a big slab you may want to rent a scarifier.

For grinding, use a walk-behind machine fitted with one or more diamond disks. Keep the grinding area wet and vacuum up the grinding slurry before it dries. Work the grinder till the whole area is smooth and even. Unless freeze-thaw caused the delamination, you can quit there. But if the original problem resulted from frost, you should probably apply a sealer to the ground-down surface. The sealer will help slow down further deterioration.

A topping is almost as much work as placing a new slab. But if you do it right it will eliminate the problem once and for all. Follow these steps:

Epoxy resin plays
a part in many slab
repairs.

1. Clean and roughen the old concrete. You may think the delamination has already left it plenty rough, but it needs more. Shot-blasting is the best choice, but scabbling or scarifying will work, too. Shot-blasting abrades the surface with steel pellets (shot). Scabbling relies on pneumatic hammers, while scarifying uses a rotating cylinder fitted with loose toothed washers that rattle around as the cylinder turns. Scarifiers are easier to find than the other choices.
2. Clean up all dust and debris, and do a thorough job. If you dropped a sandwich on the slab, would you pick it up and eat it? If not, you have more cleaning to do.
3. Soak the slab with water, and vacuum up any excess. The result should be a surface that's damp but has no ponded water.
4. Coat the slab with a paste made of cement and water, mixed to the thickness of heavy cream. Scrub the paste into the surface with a stiff broom. Don't let it dry out before moving on to the next step.
5. Pour a layer of new concrete about 3/4 in. (20 mm) thick. Use a pea-gravel mix with 3/8-in. (10-mm) coarse aggregate.
6. Finish the concrete as you like. Any finish suitable for an ordinary concrete slab will work on a concrete topping.
7. As soon as the topping is hard enough, cut it with a concrete saw directly over any joints in the base slab. If you omit this step, the topping will probably crack over the joints.
8. Cure the new concrete.

Faulted Joints

These are joints where one side has shifted up or down relative to the other side, leaving a lip or step. Faulted joints can trip pedestrians, and they look terrible under floorcoverings such as vinyl tile or thin carpet. Faulting can also occur at cracks, with the same effects and the same remedies.

If the step is up to 1/2 in. (12 mm) high, you can grind it down. Unless you have hours to spare, use a grinder with a diamond disk. Diamonds cost a lot, but they grind many times faster than abrasive blocks.

If the step is over 1/2 in. (12 mm) high, grinding will take too long, even with a diamond disk. Use a scarifier instead. If the slab has a smooth finish, you may need to finish up with a grinder. But if the slab has a float or broom finish, you may find that the scarifier leaves a surface you can live with. The repaired area will look different, but it will still be suitable for foot traffic and vehicles.

Local governments sometimes condemn sidewalks for faulted joints. The officials may tell you to replace the sidewalk. But they will usually accept grinding or scarification instead.

Settlement & Heaving

Settlement occurs when the sub-grade cannot support the weight of the slab and whatever goes on top of the slab. Heaving occurs when the subgrade expands, pushing the slab up. Expansive clay soils cause heaving when they get wet. Many kinds of soil can cause heaving if they freeze when wet. Tree roots can cause heaving, too.

Structural failures like this heaving may call for slab replacement, but most defects don't.

Settlement and heaving are among the hardest slab problems to solve because the source of the trouble lies hidden beneath the concrete. One remedy for settled slabs is to pump grout underneath, a process called mudjacking or slabjacking. It works, but it doesn't always last. Grout injection can't reverse heaving, however. Where heaving is severe, you may have no choice but to remove and replace the slab.

Structural Failure Under Load

Most cracks in concrete slabs result from shrinkage, and they don't lead to slab failure. But there are other, more serious kinds of cracks. The worst cracks occur when a slab is simply not strong enough to support the loads you put on it. The cause is usually a too-thin slab, but weak concrete can also contribute.

Normal shrinkage cracks are self-limiting. The cracks relieve stress, and the slab doesn't crack any more. In contrast, structural cracks can go on till your slab has disintegrated to gravel.

If the structural cracks came from a one-time event that is not likely to recur, you can safely glue them closed with a low-viscosity epoxy. But if your slab is cracking under everyday, recurring loads, it's probably time to replace it.

FLATWORK

INDEX

CONCRETE

INDEX

CORE COLLECTION 2009